The Growth and Influence of Islam
In the Nations of Asia and Central Asia

Tajikistan

The Growth and Influence of Islam

IN THE NATIONS OF ASIA AND CENTRAL ASIA

The Growth and Influence of Islam
In the Nations of Asia and Central Asia

Tajikistan

Colleen O'Dea

Mason Crest Publishers
Philadelphia

Produced by OTTN Publishing, Stockton, New Jersey

Mason Crest Publishers
370 Reed Road
Broomall, PA 19008
www.masoncrest.com

First printing

1 3 5 7 9 8 6 4 2

Library of Congress Cataloging-in-Publication Data

O'Dea, Colleen.
  Tajikistan / Colleen O'Dea.
      p. cm. — (The growth and influence of Islam
 in the nations of Asia and Central Asia)
 Includes bibliographical references and index.
 ISBN 1-59084-885-3
 1. Tajikistan—Juvenile literature. I. Title. II. Series.
 DK923.O33 2005
 958.6—dc22
                                    2004019830

Table of Contents

Dr. Harvey Sicherman, president and director of the Foreign Policy Research Institute, is the author of such books as *America the Vulnerable: Our Military Problems and How to Fix Them* (2002) and *Palestinian Autonomy, Self-Government and Peace* (1993).

Introduction

by Dr. Harvey Sicherman

America's triumph in the Cold War promised a new burst of peace and prosperity. Indeed, the decade between the demise of the Soviet Union and the destruction of September 11, 2001, proved deceptively hopeful. Today, of course, we are more fully aware—to our sorrow—of the dangers and troubles no longer just below the surface.

The Muslim identities of most of the terrorists at war with the United States have also provoked great interest in Islam as well as the role of religion in politics. It is crucial for Americans not to assume that Osama bin Laden's ideas are identical to those of most Muslims or, for that matter, that most Muslims are Arabs. A truly world religion, Islam claims hundreds of millions of adherents, from every ethnic group scattered across the globe. This book series covers the growth and influence of Muslims in Asia and Central Asia.

A glance at the map establishes the extraordinary coverage of our authors. Every climate and terrain may be found, along with every form of human society, from the nomadic groups of the Central Asian steppes to highly sophisticated cities such as Singapore, New Delhi, and Shanghai. The economies of the nations examined in this series are likewise highly diverse. In some, barter systems are still used; others incorporate modern stock markets. In some of the countries, large oil reserves hold out the prospect of prosperity. Other countries, such as India and China, have progressed by moving from a government-controlled to a more market-based economic system. Still other countries have built wealth on service and shipping.

Central Asia and Asia is a heavily armed and turbulent area. Three of its states (China, India, and Pakistan) are nuclear powers, and one (Kazakhstan) only recently rid itself of nuclear weapons. But it is also a place where the horse and mule remain indispensable instruments of war. All of the region's states have an extensive history of conflict, domestic and international, old and new. Afghanistan, for example, has known little but invasion and civil war over the past two decades.

Governments include dictatorships, democracies, and hybrids without a name; centralized and decentralized administrations; and older patterns of tribal and clan associations. The region is a veritable encyclopedia of political expression.

Although such variety defies easy generalities, it is still possible to make several observations. First, the geopolitics of Central Asia and Asia reflect the impact of empires and the struggles of post-imperial independence. Central Asia, a historic corridor for traders and soldiers, was the scene of Russian expansion well into Soviet times. While Kazakhstan's leaders participated in the historic meeting of December 25, 1991, that dissolved the Soviet Union, the rest of the region's newly independent republics hardly expected it. They have found it difficult to grapple with a sometimes tenuous independence, buffeted by a strong residual Russian influence, the absence of settled institutions, the temptation of newly valuable natural resources, and mixed populations lacking a solid national identity. The shards of the Soviet Union have often been sharp—witness the Russian war in Chechnya—and sometimes fatal for those ambitious to grasp them.

President Imomali Rahmonov of Tajikistan shakes hands with Russian President Vladimir Putin during a meeting in the Black Sea resort of Sochi in June 2004. Although Tajikistan became independent in September 1991, it has remained closely tied to Russia.

Moving further east, one encounters an older devolution, that of the half-century since the British Raj dissolved into India and Pakistan (the latter giving violent birth to Bangladesh in 1971). Only recently, partly under the impact of the war on terrorism, have these nuclear-armed neighbors and adversaries found it possible to renew attempts at reconciliation. Still further east, Malaysia shares a British experience, but Indonesia has been influenced by its Dutch heritage. Even China defines its own borders along the lines of the Qing empire (the last pre-republican dynasty) at its most expansionist (including Tibet and Taiwan). These imperial histories lie heavily upon the politics of the region.

A second aspect worth noting is the variety of economic experimentation afoot in the area. State-dominated economic strategies, still in the ascendant, are separating government from the actual running of commerce and industry. "Privatization," however, is frequently a byword for crony capitalism and corruption. Yet in dynamic economies such as that of China, as well as an increasingly productive India, hundreds of millions of people have dramatically improved both their standard of living and their hope for the future. All of them aspire to benefit from international trade. Competitive advantages, such as low-cost labor (in some cases trained in high technology) and valuable natural resources (oil, gas, and minerals), promise much. This is indeed a revolution of rising expectations, some of which are being satisfied.

Yet more than corruption threatens this progress. Population increase, even though moderating, still overwhelms educational and employment opportunities. Many countries are marked by extremes of wealth and poverty, especially between rural and urban areas. Dangerous jealousies threaten ethnic groups (such as anti-Chinese violence in Indonesia). Hopelessly overburdened public services portend turmoil. Public health, never adequate, is harmed further by environmental damage to critical resources (such as the Aral Sea). By and large, Central Asian and Asian countries are living well beyond their infrastructures.

Third and finally, Islam has deeply affected the states and peoples of the region. Indonesia is the largest Muslim state in the world, and India hosts the second-largest Muslim population. Islam is not only the official religion of many states, it is the very reason for Pakistan's existence. But Islamic practices and groups vary: the well-known Sunni and Shiite groups are joined by energetic Salafi (Wahabi) and Sufi movements. Over the last 20 years especially, South and Central Asia have become battlegrounds for competing Shiite (Iranian) and Wahabi (Saudi) doctrines, well financed from abroad and aggressively antagonistic toward non-Muslims and each other. Resistance to the Soviet invasion of Afghanistan brought these groups battle-tested warriors and organizers. The war on terrorism has exposed just how far-reaching and active the new advocates of holy war (jihad) can be. Indonesia, in particular, is the scene of rivalry between an older, tolerant Islam and the jihadists. But Pakistan also faces an Islamic identity crisis. And India, wracked by sectarian strife, must hold together its democratic framework despite Muslim and Hindu extremists. This newly significant struggle within Islam, superimposed on an older Muslim history, will shape political and economic destinies throughout the region and beyond. Hence, the focus of our series.

We hope that these books will enlighten both teacher and student about a critical subject in a critical area of the world. Central Asia and Asia would be important in their own right to Americans; arguably, after 9/11, they became vital to our national security. And the enduring impact of Islam is a crucial factor we must understand. We at the Foreign Policy Research Institute hope these books will illuminate both the facts and the prospects.

This grave of a victim of Tajikistan's civil war is located in Qurghonteppa. The violent conflict between supporters of Tajikistan's government and an opposition composed of Islamic and secular pro-democracy groups began in 1992. It escalated into a civil war in which approximately 60,000 people were killed before a cease-fire agreement was reached in 1997.

1

Place in the World

The Republic of Tajikistan (Jumhurii Tojikiston in the Tajik language) is a small, oddly shaped country located near the center of Asia. The country is very poor, and until recently it was of little interest to the Western world. Engineers knew that the world's tallest dam could be found in Tajikistan, and mountain climbers recognized it as the location of some of the world's highest peaks. People interested in international affairs knew that between 1992 and 1997 the country was embroiled in a bloody civil war during which approximately 60,000 Tajikistanis were killed. Otherwise, the country was rarely in the news.

Central Asia, where Tajikistan is located, has been an important region throughout human history.

People have lived in this area for millennia, and its recorded history dates back more than 2,500 years. The fabled Silk Road, an ancient trading route that connected China to Europe, passed through the region. Because of its strategic location, such conquerors as Alexander the Great and Genghis Khan have fought for control over Central Asia.

For centuries the Tajikistan region was under the control of various empires. The Persians had great influence on the development of Central Asian culture—Islam spread to Tajikistan from Persia, and the Tajik language is a variation of Persian. (By contrast, the people of other Central Asian states like Uzbekistan, Kazakhstan, Kyrgyzstan, and Turkmenistan speak Turkic languages.) Turkic and Mongol influences affected the society of the region as well. During most of the 20th century Tajikistan was part of a much different empire—the Soviet Union. It did not become an independent country until the U.S.S.R. collapsed in December 1991.

After independence, Tajikistan faced many problems. It remains one of the 20 poorest nations in the world, and the abject poverty experienced by most people, exacerbated periodically by droughts and earthquakes, forced Tajikistan to beg for humanitarian aid. Although Tajikistan received some financial assistance from other countries and from such organizations as the International Federation of Red Cross and Red Crescent Societies and the Aga Khan Foundation, its troubles were never widely publicized in the United States before 2001.

A Strategic U.S. Ally

Tajikistan became more important to the United States after September 11, 2001, when terrorists attacked the World Trade Center in New York City and the Pentagon building near Washington, D.C. The Central Asian country was strategically significant because its neighbor Afghanistan had harbored the al-Qaeda terrorist organization that carried out the attacks. Tajikistan not only shares a 749-mile-long (1,206-km-long) border with

Afghanistan, the country's government had also supported the Northern Alliance, a group of Afghan insurgents that had been trying to oust Afghanistan's **Taliban** government from power. When the United States sought support for its invasion of Afghanistan, which was intended to overthrow the Taliban and root out the al-Qaeda terrorists, Tajikistan's government quickly got behind the effort.

After agreeing in October 2001 to allow U.S.–led troops to use its airports and its airspace, Tajikistan started receiving additional aid from the United States. A year later, Tajikistan President Imomali Rahmonov (in

President Rahmonov (left) welcomes U.S. Secretary of Defense Donald Rumsfeld (center) to the presidential palace in Dushanbe, November 2001. The officials were meeting to discuss the "war on terrorism" in the wake of the September 11 attack by Islamic radicals on the United States.

Russian, Emomali Rakhmonov; throughout this book Tajik spellings of names will be used, with the Russian spelling in parentheses, where necessary) traveled to Washington, D.C., to meet with President George W. Bush. As the countries have gotten closer, Rahmonov also has hosted several meetings with high-ranking U.S. officials.

In 2003, the U.S. committed to financing the construction of a bridge between Tajikistan and Afghanistan, saying it was helping to reopen an old world trade route. This marked a major shift in U.S. foreign policy, as previously the United States had been content to let Russia influence the countries of Central Asia.

The closer ties between Tajikistan and the United States have created some tension between Tajikistan and Russia. Of all the former Soviet republics in Central Asia, Tajikistan had arguably remained closest to its former overseer. Russia's troops had helped restore order—and ensure victory by the leadership faction it wanted—during the civil war that followed Tajikistan's independence. Thousands of Russian troops remain in the country. Although the government claims they are there to stem widespread drug smuggling, many independent observers believe the troops remain to maintain Russian influence over the region.

Religious and Economic Concerns

Although Islam is the dominant religion of Tajikistan, most Tajikistani Muslims do not wish to strictly apply religious laws to government and other areas of life. While Tajikistan does have a legitimate Islamic political party—unlike its neighbors, which have forbidden such groups—the government is secular, and most people do not want to be governed by a theocracy like Iran's.

Still, religion has the potential to be a volatile issue. The Taliban may be gone from Afghanistan, but Central Asia is home to other Islamist groups whose activites include terrorism. In early 2004, Tajikistan's neighbor

Uzbekistan suffered deadly terrorist bombings. However, some experts believe Tajikistan's leaders have inflated the threat of Islamic radicals to justify political repression of opposition groups and maintain their own hold on power.

A movement like Islamism may one day appeal to the people of Tajikistan because of the country's widespread poverty. Approximately 80 percent of Tajikistanis earn less than $300 a year. Although government officials say they are trying to improve the situation, there has been little economic reform to date. A select few have become rich, thanks to arrangements with corrupt politicians in which they took over ownership of state-run industries. Overall, however, two in five workers are unemployed. Because there are so few job opportunities, each year tens of thousands of Tajikistani workers travel to Russia to find menial jobs.

When the Soviet Union ruled Tajikistan, it provided money for social services. Schools and medical centers had adequate books and supplies, although the level of services were not up to the standards of the Western world, or even of other republics within the Soviet Union. Unfortunately, since Tajikistan became independent in 1991, the quality and availability of these services have deteriorated.

But the country is still in its infancy, especially considering its civil war only ended in 1997. If Tajikistan is able to develop its economy and increase trade, it could improve the standard of living for its citizens. More assistance from the U.S. and other countries, then, is welcome. At the same time, the United States now sees the value of being involved in Central Asia, and helping the former Soviet republics develop is one way the U.S. can keep Islamist extremists from gaining a foothold in the region. Because of the growing importance of Tajikistan, this is the perfect time to shed some light on this small but strategically important nation.

The Khawag River runs through mountainous territory on the border of Tajikistan and Afghanistan.

2

The Land

ajikistan is a study in contrasts. It contains some of the highest mountain peaks in Central Asia, as well as deep river valleys. An abundance of wildlife lives in the lush forests, but the country also contains arid deserts swept by periodic dust storms. In some areas water gushes through numerous rivers; in others, it is frozen in huge mountain *glaciers*. Some of the lowlands, especially in the southwestern part of the country, get almost no rain even in a normal year, and have warm temperatures, while the highest peaks are frigid and snow-covered year-round.

The smallest country in Central Asia, Tajikistan comprises only 55,251 square miles (143,100 square kilometers). That's about the size of the state of Wisconsin or the country of Greece. Most of its land is not suitable for agriculture. It is either mountainous—

more than half of the country rises at least 9,800 feet (3,000 meters) above sea level—or desert.

Tajikistan is landlocked, meaning it has no coastline. The closest large body of water is the Aral Sea, to the northwest in Central Asia. But this sea is in danger—it has been shrinking due to diversions of water from its river tributaries for irrigation. Two rivers that flow through Tajikistan, the Syr Dar'ya and the Amu Dar'ya (the word *dar'ya* means "river"), are among its tributaries, so Tajikistan has agreed to join other nations in the Aral basin in an effort to save the sea. However, little of value has come from that effort so far, and the sea continues to shrink at a rate of about 23 square miles (60 sq km) a year.

Local officials are concerned about the state of the environment within Tajikistan. Working with the United Nations, they have published several "State of the Environment" reports over the years. These reports outline environmental pressures and concerns and the actions needed to protect natural resources.

Regions in Tajikistan

The wondrous mountains and glaciers of Tajikistan are located in the Kuhistoni Badakhshon (better known as the Gorno-Badakhshan Autonomous Province), one of four administrative regions into which the country is divided. Kuhistoni Badakhshon is the largest *viloyat*, or province, in physical size. Located in the east, it comprises almost half of Tajikistan's land, but contains less than 5 percent of its population. China and Afghanistan are its neighbors. Khorugh (Khorog) on the Afghanistan border, is its capital city.

The northernmost province is Sughd, which is also sometimes known by the name of its main city, Khujand (Khodjent). This area covers the fertile Fergana Valley, so it is an agricultural center.

In the southwest, the administrative division is called Khatlon viloyat.

The Geography of Tajikistan

Location: Central Asia, west of China

Area: About the size of Wisconsin

    Total: 55,251 square miles (143,100 square kilometers)

    Land: 55,097 square miles (142,700 sq km)

    Water: 154 square miles (400 sq km)

Borders: Total, 2,269 miles (3,651 kilometers); Afghanistan, 749 miles (1,206 km); China, 257 miles (414 km); Kyrgyzstan, 541 miles (870 km); Uzbekistan, 721 miles (1,161 km)

Climate: midlatitude continental, hot summers, mild winters; semiarid to polar in Pamir Mountains

Terrain: Pamir and Alai (Alay) Mountains dominate landscape; western Fergana Valley in north, Kofarnihon and Vakhsh Valleys in southwest

Elevation extremes:

    lowest point—Syr Dar'ya (Sirdaryo) 984 feet (300 meters)

    highest point—Qullohi Ismoili Somoni, 24,590 feet (7,495 m)

Natural hazards: Earthquakes and floods

Source: CIA World Factbook, 2004

Its major city is Qurghonteppa, (Kurgan-tiube). Nearly all the people there rely on agriculture for their livelihoods but farms sometimes fail because of drought.

In the center and west of the country are a group of cities and villages that are not part of a specific administrative division. Instead, they are simply called "regions under republican administration," meaning the national government rules these areas directly. This includes the capital city of Dushanbe, which is the administrative center of this area, as well as the Qarotegin (Karategin) and Hisor (Gissar) valleys and the Kofarnihon area.

Tajikistan is oddly shaped, as one look at a map of its borders shows. The Fergana Valley juts north between Uzbekistan and Kyrgyzstan. A small triangle of land projects from the tip of the Isfara Valley into Kyrgyzstan. Both Kyrgyzstan and Uzbekistan also used to be Soviet republics before the breakup of the U.S.S.R. To the east, massive China looms along the border. To the south, Afghanistan humps up, narrowing the center of Tajikistan.

Forests

Although forests are not numerous in the country, the forests of Tajikistan are very important because so much of the land is mountainous. Between 3 percent and 3.5 percent of the country's land is forested. That's only about a third of what it was 70 years ago. Industrialization and the expansion of agriculture—both results of Soviet rule—have contributed to the country's **deforestation**. As a result, the nation has been facing more landslides, avalanches, and floods than in the past. And, as part of a vicious cycle, those natural phenomena wind up destroying more forestland: up to 988 acres (400 hectares) each year.

While there is relatively little forestland in the country, some 200 species of trees and bushes can be found in Tajikistan. Different species are found in different types of forests. The country's forests can be divided into six main types. Juniper forests, named for the evergreen trees that predominate, take up the most area, about 370,000 acres (150,000 hectares). They grow at altitudes as high as 12,000 feet (3,700 meters). In addition to numerous species of evergreen junipers, the forests also support honeysuckle, dog rose, and other bushes and herbs. The large root systems of these plants help prevent soil from washing out as rain flows down the sides of mountains.

Tugai forests are typically found along the banks of rivers. These encompass areas where water changes to sand or mud, then to reeds, then to thick tree growth, then to sparser shrub cover and ultimately to desert. In Tajikistan, these are found in the lowlands, where it is hot and wet, especially in the lower Vakhsh River region. Tugai forests have high groundwater levels and typically flood during the rainy season. Poplar, oleaster, and tamarisk trees are common.

At higher altitudes, along the ridges of such mountain ranges as the Hisor, are broad-leaf forests. Such moisture-loving trees as walnut, maple, and apple thrive here. Rose bushes also can be found growing among the trees. These forests are key to regulating the runoff from rain. They also are an important source of timber and home to 40 species of mammals, 200 species of birds, and 10 species of reptiles.

Small-leaf forests are found at heights of between 7,500 and 11,000 feet (2,300 and 3,500 meters) in mountain river areas. White willow, birch, and poplar species predominate. These forests help protect riverbanks and prevent **mudflows**.

Xerophytic light forests are found mainly in the south, at heights of between 2,000 and 5,500 feet (600 and 1,700 meters). Xerophytic plants are those that have adapted to an area with little water. More than three quarters of these forests are pistachio forests, making up almost 150,000 acres (72,000 hectares). They have declined dramatically—pistachio forests covered 420,077 acres (170,000 hectares) in 1932. Almond and pomegranate are the other dominant trees in these forests. These forests also protect the soil and prevent mudflows.

The final type is the desert, or saxaul, forests, which also are found in the south. The white saxaul, or salt tree, and black saxaul both are evergreens that can grow to be 100 years old. These trees help stabilize sandy soils and they serve as pasturelands in the spring and fall.

Tajikistan's terrain encourages cattle grazing. But at the same time, grazing is one of the main problems facing the forests today. At least 7 of every 10 acres of forestlands are used for agriculture, so it is difficult for authorities to protect the trees and help increase the amount of forestland.

Deserts

Much of the land in Tajikistan is considered to be desert. The sandiest land is in the hot deserts in the south. Sandy deserts are found at between 1,300 feet and 2,000 feet (about 400 and 610 meters) above sea level. There are also mountain deserts in Tajikistan, at between 11,500 and 15,000 feet (3,530 and 4,600 meters). These are located in the eastern Pamir Mountains. As much as 40 percent of the East Pamir region is considered natural desert, because it receives so little annual precipitation.

Historically, due to its geography and climate, the country has had natural deserts. However, the improper irrigation of crops and overcutting of

A woman walks through barren land near Shahrtuz in southern Tajikistan. A massive drought in the region during 2000 and 2001 turned farmland of marginal quality into dusty desert throughout the country.

forests over time are contributing to the ***desertification*** of even more land. This is a phenomenon about which environmentalists are concerned, because there already is so little ***arable*** land in Tajikistan.

Severe droughts in the early 21st century exacerbated the aridness of some of the dry areas, turning them into Sahara-like deserts. David Shukman, world affairs correspondent for the BBC, visited southern Tajikistan to investigate the consequences of the drought—including some 1 million Tajiks facing starvation—in October 2001. "Until I visited the barren wheatfields of southern Tajikistan, I never really knew what the term 'dustbowl' meant," he reported from Kulob (Kulyab). "But around the town of Kulyab, I saw mile after mile of desert landscape. Clods of earth looked like rubble. Huge swirling clouds of dust powered through the valleys. The dust-devils looked nothing less than evil."

Because so much of the land is so harsh, most of the country's people live in two centers—in lowlands in the extreme north and south. Several impressive mountain ranges separate these population centers.

Dividing Mountains

Three mountain ranges separate the northern and southern lowlands. These are the Turkestan, Zarafshon, and Hisor chains, which are extended from the Alai mountain range that runs across southern Kyrgyzstan. The mountains of the Zarafshon chain reach 18,012 feet (5,490 meters) into the sky. In the Turkestan range, the highest peak is about 18,077 feet (5,510 meters) above sea level. The Hisor has the highest peak of the three ranges; its tallest point is 18,176 feet (5,540 meters).

These mountains separate Dushanbe and southern Tajikistan from the Fergana Valley, which has the most productive farmland, in the north. This valley crosses into Uzbekistan and Kyrgyzstan north of Tajikistan. The land there is so fertile that Fergana is the most densely populated region in all of Central Asia. Helping make the land so productive is the

Syr Dar'ya, which runs through the length of the valley. About 121 miles (195 km) of the river's 1,491 miles (2,400 km) run through Tajikistan before eventually feeding into the Aral Sea.

The other major population center is in the southwest and includes the capital, Dushanbe. Located in the lush Hisor valley, the capital is bisected by the north-south running Varzob River. The river provides drinking water to the people there. Originating in the glaciers of the Hisor Mountains, the Varzob also helps irrigate croplands outside the city. It flows for 44 miles (71 km).

But while these mountains are impressive enough, there are larger and more imposing peaks in the east. The biggest and most daunting mountains in Tajikistan are the Pamirs, which dominate the eastern half of the country. Called *Bam-i Dunya* ("the roof of the world") by locals and mountaineers, the Pamir Mountains dwarf almost every other mountain range in the world outside of the Himalayas in Nepal. Their snow-capped peaks gleam in the sunlight as they reach up into the wisps of white clouds that pass across their highest peaks.

The Pamirs contain the country's highest point, Qullohi Ismoili Somoni. It was originally known as Garmo Peak, but in the 1930s the Soviet government changed its name to Stalin Peak, after Soviet leader Joseph Stalin. In 1962, after the end of Stalin's regime, it was renamed Communism Peak. It was given a Tajik name in 1998. Qullohi Ismoili Somoni reaches 24,590 feet (7,495 meters) high, making it one of the highest places on earth. Qullohi Ismoili Somoni is craggy and ice-covered, even though the land over which it towers tends to be dry and bare.

As Tajikistan puts its civil war further behind it, more hikers are traversing the Pamirs. Numerous trekking routes are being publicized throughout the Kuhistoni Badakhshon region where the Pamirs are located. Vladimir Ratzek, a Russian mountaineer, wrote an essay in which he contemplated the reasons that drive people to trek through the Pamirs. "Why would one wish

Mountain climbers attempt to scale a peak in the Pamir Mountains of eastern Tajikistan. These ice-covered mountains contain the country's highest point, Qullohi Ismoili Somoni.

to travel on foot in this uninhabited mountain region with its hazards of sudden blizzards, avalanches, rock falls, crevasses, accidents, sunburn, frostbite, and all forms of high altitude illness?" wrote Ratzek. "[B]ecause it is difficult, interesting, beautiful, expansive and evocative of all of one's physical and mental powers and because nature there, though sparse in plant and animal life, is of a special kind in this kingdom of crags, ice and snow."

The Pamir Highway stretches through the mountain range. This route is the only way through the mountains and allows passage north to Kyrgyzstan and south to Khorugh on the Afghanistan border. The road is believed to have once been part of the Silk Road, the ancient network of trade routes that linked China and the civilizations of the Mediterranean Sea.

In the mountains live sheep—including the famous Marco Polo sheep, which have huge, curling horns—and rare snow leopards, but few people. Many gorges and canyons cut through the mountains. The Pamir region contains many wide green valleys, but they tend to be treeless. There are also numerous glaciers which, when they melt in the summer, feed the streams and rivers that irrigate farmland in the lower valleys.

Ice and Running Water

As if hosting some of the highest peaks in the world wasn't enough, the Pamir Mountains also are home to many glaciers, huge masses of ice that move slowly and are thousands of years old. In some places, the ice is nearly 500 feet (150 meters) thick. The Fedchenko Glacier is about 48 miles (77 km) long and covers more than 270 square miles (700 sq km). In addition to Fedchenko, numerous other glaciers make up the Pamir glacial field. Glaciers cover about 6 percent of Tajikistan's total area.

Studies show that the country's glaciers are shrinking, probably because of rising temperatures and a decrease in precipitation. Runoff from melting glaciers during the warmest months (June, July, and August) and the geography of the mountainous areas have created an abundant network of 947 rivers and 1,300 lakes. In many cases, Tajikistan's rivers are the only source of drinking water for those communities located along the riverbanks.

The country's largest lake is Lake Qarokul (Karakul) in the Eastern Pamirs. Qarokul (which means "black lake") stretches across 94,000 acres (more than 38,000 hectares). Some believe the lake basin is a crater formed by an ancient meteorite impact. Although the lake is located at 12,840 feet (3,914 meters) above sea level, its water is salty.

Tajikistan's deepest freshwater lake is Sarez Lake, in the steep canyon of the Bartang River in the western Pamirs. It is located at a height of 10,630 feet (3,240 meters) above sea level. The lake was formed in 1911 when a major landslide in the canyon created a natural dam. It covers 33 square miles (86 sq km), and is 1,608 feet (490 meters) deep.

Tajikistan has nine reservoirs, which are used primarily to generate electricity, irrigate crops, breed fish, and supply drinking water. More than 95 percent of the country's electricity is generated by hydroelectric power plants. The largest reservoirs are Qairoqqum (Kairakkum) in the north and Norak (Nurek) in the central part of the country.

Climate

Tajikistan has what is known as a continental climate, meaning that winter temperatures are cool enough to support a period of stable snow cover while a moderate amount of rain falls during the warmer summers. This is similar to the climate of other countries in the Northern Hemisphere, such as Russia and the midwestern United States. The temperature and amount of precipitation vary widely depending on the region and altitude. For instance, the average air temperature in the south is about 63° Fahrenheit (17° Celsius), while in the eastern Pamirs the average temperature sinks as low as 19° F (−7° C).

July is the warmest month throughout the land. The average temperature is 86° F (30° C) in the lowlands. Likewise, January is the coldest month. In January, temperatures in the Eastern Pamirs average 0° F (−18° C), but they can drop lower. Although the lowlands like the Fergana Valley are shielded from the coldest winds, temperatures there drop below freezing about 100 days each year.

On average the country receives between 28 and 63 inches (71 and 160 centimeters) of rain or snow each year. But the hot, dry deserts in the south and cold high-mountain deserts in the Eastern Pamirs get as little as 6 inches (15 cm) of precipitation a year. Yet the Fedchenko Glacier, also in the Pamir Mountains, receives as much as 88 inches (224 cm) of mostly frozen precipitation annually. Most of the rain and snow falls in winter and spring.

Earthquakes and Mudslides

A lot of rain falling on steep slopes that are not protected by the roots of trees or grasses, added to cascading streams of water released by the summer glacial melts, can lead to mudslides. Some of these prove deadly. According to Tajikistan's 2002 "State of the Environment Report," every year the country sees numerous landslides, mudflows, and avalanches. Overgrazing on some slopes has left the mountainous regions, particularly in the Hisor-Alai ranges, particularly vulnerable.

A satellite view of Sarez Lake, which is surrounded by glacier-covered mountains. The lake was created by an earthquake, which formed a natural dam, pictured at the center of this photo. Scientists fear that one day another earthquake could cause it to overflow and flood the Bartang, Panj, and Amu rivers. This would have catastrophic consequences for communities in Tajikistan and other countries, so the United Nations and other organizations are monitoring the situation closely.

One of the worst recent instances occurred in August 2002 in Kuhistoni Badakhshon. That mudslide, which hit the village of Dasht near Khorugh, left 24 people dead. It also led to a large number of injuries, the collapse of 75 homes, and the deaths of livestock. The mudslide damaged bridges, roads, a medical center, a school, a library, and some communications infrastructure. More than 500 people had to be resettled in a new village.

Because a fault runs underneath the country, Tajikistan is prone to earthquakes. The country experienced at least three quakes during 2002–03. In the worst recent earthquake, in January 2002, three people died and six were injured in an area east of Dushanbe. That quake also destroyed 110 homes.

Earthquakes sometimes also cause mudslides—a deadly combination that can wipe out entire villages. For instance, a January 1989 earthquake in the Hisor region killed 274 people and caused mudslides that buried three villages.

In rainy years, floods are another problem. A May 1992 flood killed 1,346 people, one of the worst disasters in Tajikistan's history.

In the 2002 environmental report, Tajikistan government officials blamed an increasing number of natural disasters during the 1990s to the loss of forestlands. They are working to protect trees and growth along the mountains as a way to prevent mudslides and other disasters, as well as to provide a better overall environment for the people.

Pro-government soldiers ride a tank in Vakhch, Tajikistan, during the country's 1992–97 civil war.

3

The History

The word *Tajikistan* means "land of the Tajiks." However, before the 20th century there was no such place as Tajikistan. The ethnic group today known as Tajiks did not always refer to themselves by this name; *Tajik* was a somewhat-derogatory term used by other Central Asian peoples, particularly Turks and Pashtuns, to refer to those people who spoke Persian. The borders of Tajikistan were not established until 1924, when it was part of the Soviet Union; the country did not become independent until 1991.

The ancestors of the modern Tajik ethnic group are believed to be Iranian people who migrated into Central Asia during the seventh and sixth centuries B.C. They lived in a region that stretched from what today is northern Afghanistan to north of the Syr Dar'ya, and established two states in this region.

Soghdiana included the northern area of modern Tajikistan, as well as the cities of Samarqand (Samarkand) and Bukhara, which today are inside the borders of Uzbekistan. Another state, Bactria, was located in the southern part of Tajikistan and northern Afghanistan.

The independence of Bactria and Soghdiana was relatively short-lived, as larger and stronger regional powers sought to incorporate the territories into their empires. In the sixth century B.C. most of the Tajikistan region fell under the control of Cyrus the Great's Achaemenid Persian Empire. Two centuries later, the armies of Macedonian conqueror Alexander the Great defeated the Achaemenids and incorporated Persian territories into his vast empire. After 18 months of fighting, Alexander's soldiers defeated the Sogdians in 327 B.C.; he eventually pushed as far east as Khujand in northern Tajikistan.

To solidify his position in the region and gain support from Central Asian tribal leaders, Alexander married Roxana, the daughter of a member of the Sogdian nobility, and established at least 10 cities where his armies were based. Among these was a city called Alexandria-Eschate (meaning "Alexandria the furthermost"), near Khujand in the Fergana Valley.

Trade and Conquest

The conquests of Alexander had a powerful influence on the region. They introduced the philosophy, learning, art, and culture of the Greek world to the people of Central Asia, while exposing the Western world to the riches of the East. This would contribute to an increased desire for trade between Asia and Europe that would outlast Alexander's empire, which disintegrated soon after his death in 323 B.C. Six of Alexander's generals fought over control of the Macedonian empire. Two smaller empires eventually coalesced, one in the Middle East and Central Asia ruled by the Seleucid dynasty, the other in Egypt ruled by the Ptolemaic dynasty.

The Tajikistan region was initially part of the Seleucid kingdom, but around 250 B.C. the Seleucid governor of Bactria, Diodotos I, declared the region an independent kingdom. For about 80 years the Bactrians were a strong regional power, but the kingdom became divided and part of it was returned to Seleucid control. Eventually, Bactria fell under the control of the Kushan Empire, which was based in India. The region was under Kushan domination from the first to the fourth centuries A.D.

By the first century B.C., a network of trade routes had been established to link China with the Roman Empire, which had supplanted the Greeks as the dominant power in the Mediterranean region and Middle East. At least one of the many routes crossed through the territory that today is Tajikistan. Collectively, the trade routes would become known as the Silk Road, because Chinese silk, which was highly prized in Rome, was one of the main items traded. Many other goods were traded as well. Spices from China were exchanged for Roman glass and textiles. Gold, ivory, ceramics, plants, and animals were traded as well. More important, perhaps, was the exchange of knowledge, religion, and philosophy between the Eastern and Western civilizations.

This illustration shows the army of Alexander the Great stopping in Bactria to examine burning oil seeping through the ground.

In the fifth century, the Huns, a group of nomads from Central Asia, moved west toward Rome. The Huns and other "barbarian" groups pressured the western half of the Roman Empire. However, by moving west the Huns left Central Asia open to invasion by other tribes. Some of these invaders were Turkic, while others came from Mongolia, China, or other parts of Asia.

Rome eventually fell in 476 A.D., but trading along the Silk Road continued. The eastern half of the empire (based in Constantinople and known as the Byzantine Empire) would remain powerful and influential for another millennium. Over the next two centuries, the Byzantines would fight regularly with the Sassanid rulers of Persia.

The Spread of Islam

By the beginning of the eighth century, a new power had emerged in the region: the Arabs, who conquered the Sassanids and pushed back the borders of the Byzantine Empire. The Arabs had begun raiding Central Asian lands as early as 651, and by 715 they had annexed the area of modern-day Tajikistan into their empire. As the Arabs spread their influence into Central Asia, their new religion, Islam, began to supplant earlier religions, such as Nestorian Christianity and Zoroastrianism. Islam spread into Central Asia not only by conquest, but also through trade and missionary work.

In 750, a civil war among the Arabs over the leadership of the growing Islamic empire ended with the acension of the ruling Abbasid dynasty. The Abbasids set out to unify the various kingdoms and tribes of the Muslim lands as a single state under their control. Local leaders were permitted to govern the territories on behalf of the Abbasid caliphs, who directed the entire empire from their capital at Baghdad. A Persian named Saman-Khuda was given authority to rule the Tajikistan region in 819; his descendants became known as the Samanids, and under the guidance of this dynasty Bukhara became a center of trade and Islamic culture.

Pressure by invading Turkic tribes from the northeast weakened the Samanid dynasty. In 999, the Turkic Ghaznavids and Qarakhanids seized control over the region, and over the next few centuries, various Turkic groups battled for control of Central Asia. Early in the 13th century, however, a ruthless new invader swept across the grasslands from the east. The Mongols, under the warlord Genghis Khan, overran cities throughout Central Asia, including Bukhara and Samarqand. They left virtually nothing intact in their path, and killed 30,000 people during their capture of Bukhara in 1220.

The Mongols continued to move west even after the death of Genghis Khan in 1227. A Mongol army under Genghis Khan's grandson Hülegü

This 10th century Samanid mausoleum in Bukhara provides an example of the decorative brickwork common in the Islamic societies of Central Asia. Traders and missionaries brought Islam to the region less than a century after the death of the Prophet Muhammad in 632.

Khan sacked Baghdad in 1258, ending the reign of the Abbasid caliphs and destroying the Arab Islamic Empire.

Khanates of Central Asia

At its height, the Mongol Empire covered more land than any other empire in history, stretching across Asia from China to eastern Europe. However, the empire was eventually divided among the descendants of Genghis Khan, and four separate khanates, or kingdoms, were established. The Tajikistan region became part of the Ulus Chaghatai, ruled by Genghis's second son.

The Mongol conquests were very destructive. However, by the later years of Mongol rule, parts of Central Asia, including Bukhara, revived. Trade flourished, as did science and culture. In addition, there was an important difference between the Mongols and other powerful empires of the past. Previously, conquerors had imposed their culture and beliefs on the people they ruled. By contrast, the Mongols adopted the cultures of the people they conquered. One element of this was religion. By the early 14th century, the Mongol rulers had accepted Islam, the religion already practiced by most Persians.

The power of the Ulus Chaghatai waned during the 14th century. It was not until the rise of the Turkic conqueror Timur Lenk (Timur the Lame, or Tamerlane) during the late 14th century that the region was reunited. Timur had been born near Samarqand, and he made the city the center of cultural and political life for Central Asia.

After Timur's death in 1405, his empire was divided among his descendants, the Timurids. Eventually the once-powerful state became a patchwork of principalities ruled by various Timurid khans. As Timurid power waned over the next century, another Turkic group, the Uzbeks, grew stronger. From Bukhara, the Shaybani Uzbeks gradually defeated the Timurid principalities during the late 15th and early 16th centuries.

In the late 16th century, the Shaybani were replaced by another Uzbek clan, the Janids. However, the Janid dynasty lost power when a Persian army conquered Bukhara in 1740. When the Persians were ousted after 1747, various Uzbek clans battled for power. By the end of the century, these had coalesced into three distinct Uzbek kingdoms: the emirate of Bukhara and the khanates of Khiva and Kokand.

Russian Rule

By the 19th century, European powers were beginning to look toward Central Asia. The Russian czars wanted to expand their growing empire, as well as to check the spread of British power in the region. The British controlled much of South Asia. The two empires became involved in a power struggle for influence over Persia and Central Asia that became known as the "Great Game."

Russia began incorporating parts of Central Asia into its empire between 1822 and 1848, when it annexed the Kazakh lands in four stages. Russian troops captured Tashkent from the Kokand Khanate in 1866; the next year, the city became the capital of the new Guberniya (Governorate-General) of Turkestan, which included the districts of Khujand and Uroteppa in modern-day Tajikistan. By 1876, Russia had annexed the entire Kokand Khanate.

Although Russian soldiers seized Samarqand in 1868, Czar Alexander II decided not to annex the emirate of Bukhara. One reason was the emirate's symbolic importance to Muslims; the czar feared a backlash from the Islamic world if he forcibly added the territory to his empire. Also, the British viewed Bukhara as a strategic buffer between their Indian colony and the Russian empire; annexing the territory might spark a full-scale war with Great Britain. The czar instead made a treaty with Bukhara under which the emirate became a Russian protectorate. In effect, this subordinated Bukhara to Russia, although the emirate's borders were actually expanded by the treaty. The czar granted the emir control over a district that included Dushanbe (now the capital of Tajikistan), as compensation for the loss of territory in the Fergana Valley.

The Russian administration reached a similar protectorate arrangement with the khan of Khiva in 1873. In 1895, Russia gained control over the eastern Pamir Mountains. By this time, all of modern-day Tajikistan was either under direct Russian control, as part of its Turkestan colony, or under indirect control through Bukhara or Khiva.

In a day-to-day sense, life did not change much for the Tajiks under Russian rule. The same local officials continued to oversee their villages. The czarist government encouraged Russians to move into sparsely populated areas of Central Asia, but few Russians moved to the densely populated Fergana Valley. One important change was an increase in cotton cultivation in the region. The Russian government encouraged farmers to plant cotton, rather than traditional grain crops, in the Fergana Valley and Bukhara.

However, throughout Central Asia opposition to Russian influence began to grow during the late 19th century. Much of the unrest was due to social and economic strains within the traditional society, partly caused by the influx of Russian settlers. In 1885–86 Muslim peasants in the Fergana Valley revolted, and Russian troops were needed to put down the uprising. Short-lived revolts also occurred in 1910 and 1913.

In the face of Russian domination, some Tajiks turned to a movement called Jadidism. (This name is derived from *jadid*, the Arabic word for "new.") The Jadidists sought to preserve Islamic culture in Central Asia, while also promoting secular education and other reforms intended to modernize their societies. The movement's leaders were young intellectuals, many of whose families were members of the wealthy merchant class. Others were the sons of Islamic religious figures. The czarist government opposed the Jadidist movement, because it feared the Jadidists would promote independence. Russia soon cracked down on Jadidists in Turkestan. The rulers of Bukhara and Khiva followed Russia's lead, outlawing the movement and forcing dissident Jadidists into exile. Despite this, by 1914 there were underground Jadidist organizations in several cities of present-day Tajikistan.

Turmoil and the End of the Empire

Unrest against czarist rule was not limited to Central Asia. In 1905 a series of uprisings in Russia forced Czar Nicholas II to sign the October Manifesto, which promised an expansion of civil rights and a greater role for the people in political life. Although this halted much of the unrest, in practice Russian society was largely unchanged. Despite the creation of a legislature (the Duma), political power remained in the czar's hands and a relatively small number of industrialists and noble families controlled most of the empire's wealth. The reforms did little to improve the lives of most Russians, and they did nothing for Tajiks and others in Central Asia. After 1907 Turkestan was denied representation in the Duma, for example, and Central Asians were forced to pay certain taxes that Russians did not have to pay.

When World War I began in 1914, Russia entered the fighting on the side of its ally France. The Russians sought more cotton, cattle, and horses from Central Asia for its war effort. Then the czar began forcing Central Asian men to join labor crews to assist the Russian military. This led to an extensive uprising in 1916. This uprising began in the Fergana Valley and spread to Khujand and other parts of Turkestan. Although Russian troops quickly regained control of Khujand, fighting continued in other areas of Central Asia through the end of the year.

In March 1917, revolution in Russia itself led to the abdication of the unpopular Czar Nicholas II. A republic was established with a provisional government, but it had limited power or popular support. In November

1917, the Bolsheviks, led by Vladimir Lenin, overthrew the provisional government. This led to a civil war in Russia that lasted until 1921, as the **Bolshevik** Red Army battled for control with various Russian republican factions.

As it secured control over Russia, the Red Army turned to the former imperial territories. In 1920 the Red Army under General Mikhail Frunze occupied Bukhara and drove out the emir. Turkestan, including the northern part of present-day Tajikistan, was incorporated into the Russian

A truck carries Bolsheviks carrying political signs through a Moscow street, October 1917. After the last Russian czar gave up power, the Bolsheviks won a long civil war in Russia, establishing the Union of Soviet Socialist Republics in 1922.

Soviet Federated Socialist Republic (RSFSR) in 1921. The next year, Lenin announced the formation of the Union of Soviet Socialist Republics (USSR, or Soviet Union), which included the RSFSR, the Ukrainian Soviet Socialist Republic (SSR), Belorussian SSR, and Transcaucasian SSR (modern-day Georgia, Armenia, and Azerbaijan).

Although the communists had political control, they still had to contend with unrest in Central Asia over the next decade. Thousands of Central Asians organized themselves into bands of resistance fighters called **Basmachi** ("bandits") by the Russians. The Basmachi movement began in the Fergana Valley. Although resistance to the communists spread to other areas, the groups were separate and lacked overall coordination. That ultimately doomed the Basmachi cause. The Red Army took control of Dushanbe in 1921, and Basmachi south of the city were put down a year later. Most of the guerrilla fighting in the Tajikistan region ended by 1925, although some pockets of resistance remained.

Although the Red Army was much better armed than the Basmachi, not every battle was won through bloodshed. Bolshevik officials promised rebels tax relief, reversal of anti-religious policies the Bolsheviks had tried to impose, and an end to communist agricultural controls if the rebels would put down their weapons. These assurances won over some of the Basmachi, although ultimately the promises were not kept.

The Creation of Tajikistan

In 1924, the Soviet government drew new political boundaries within the Soviet Union, creating additional republics. In Central Asia, these boundaries were created to separate the major ethnic groups into their own states. The Russians justified this move by arguing that it would fulfill the nationalist sentiments of the various Central Asian peoples, and therefore reduce support for the Basmachis, while keeping the lands within the Soviet system.

The extent of nationalist feeling within the region at this time is debatable, however. Although some groups did observe ethnic differences in language and culture, few people believed ethnicity was politically relevant or expected borders to be drawn along ethnic lines. For example, the Tajik and Uzbek peoples had lived close together for centuries, could speak one another's languages, and had intermarried. Disregarding these facts, the Soviets divided the valuable Fergana Valley, populated by members of three ethnic groups (Uzbeks, Tajiks, and Kyrgyz) and among the most fertile land in Central Asia, between the new Uzbek SSR and Kirghizia, which was part of the RSFSR. Tajikistan was initially designated as an autonomous region within the Uzbek SSR; at that time it did not include land in the Fergana Valley.

During the 1920s, Joseph Stalin emerged from a power struggle to become the unchallenged leader of the USSR. Stalin wanted to discourage anything that might challenge the authority of the Soviet government. He also wanted to dilute nationalist movements, and shifted large groups of people from their homes to different parts of the Soviet Union.

In 1929, Stalin redrew the map of Central Asia again. Territory in the Fergana Valley was added to Tajikistan, then it was separated from the Uzbek SSR and given full status as an autonomous republic, the Tajik (or Tadzhik) SSR. However, cultural and population centers that historically had been important to the ethnic Tajiks, such as Samarqand and Bukhara, remained part of the Uzbek SSR. As a result, Uzbekistan has always had a large minority population of ethnic Tajiks.

The Tajik SSR became the smallest of the Soviet Union's four Central Asian republics. (A fifth republic, the Kirghiz SSR, was created in 1936.) The Soviets turned Dushanbe, a small, earthquake-plagued market town with 3,000 residents, into the capital of the Tajik SSR. Renaming it Stalinobod, the Soviets built a railroad through the city and constructed numerous light manufacturing facilities.

Problems in the Soviet Union

Under Stalin, the Soviet Union undertook several major economic changes. One was the policy of agricultural collectivization, which Stalin believed would increase farm production. Under this policy small farms would be united into larger, state-run farms, which theoretically could be run more efficiently. The state would dole out the resources produced by each farm, making sure that both the rural farmers and the industrial workers in Soviet cities would receive a fair share.

Stalin wanted farmers in Central Asia to concentrate on cultivating cotton, rather than on food crops. Their cotton could be shipped to factories in the European parts of the USSR, where it could be turned into finished goods. The farmers would be fed with their share of the crops grown in other parts of the Soviet Union.

Collectivism ultimately proved to be a disastrous policy. In practice, the quotas set by the Soviet government were so high that many farmers saw their standard of living drop dramatically. Because Soviet economic planners did not place a high value on cotton and other raw materials, the Tajik SSR's contribution to the Soviet economy was undervalued. Farmers throughout the USSR slaughtered their animals or destroyed their grain in protest, rather than joining collective farms. This resulted in a severe national drop in agricultural productivity, and contributed to a disastrous famine in 1932–33 in which an estimated 5 million people died.

Stalin used harsh measures to force the peasants to accept his collectivization program. Soviet officials arrested peasants who refused to turn their land over to collectives; some were executed, while others were sent to labor camps. When communists in the Tajik SSR protested against high production quotas, Stalin expelled thousands of them from the Communist Party. By 1939, virtually every high-ranking government position in the republic was held by a Russian, rather than an ethnic Tajik, and 90 percent of Soviet agriculture was collectivized.

Some of the changes instituted as a result of Soviet rule benefited the new republic. The overall standard of living in the Tajik SSR, which had been very low before the Soviet era, rose as cotton cultivation was modernized and expanded. Both the health care and educational systems improved, too. By the late 1980s, almost everyone could read and write. Still, the Tajik SSR was the poorest of the Soviet republics, and the quality of health care and education was not as good as in Russia or most of the other Soviet republics.

Stalin and other Communists also attempted to eliminate religious practices within the Soviet Union and create a society that was officially atheistic. During the 1930s the Soviets embarked on a major campaign against Islam in the Tajik SSR and other Central Asian republics. Islamic schools were closed, and Muslims who refused to give up their religion were arrested and exiled or executed. Government officials refused to allow people to make a pilgrimage to the city

The slogan on this Soviet propaganda poster from 1931 reads, "The fight for the Bolshevik harvesting of the crop is the fight for socialism." Tajiks and other people in Central Asia resisted Stalin's policy of forcing Soviet peasants onto collective farms, but this resulted in persecution and a distastrous famine.

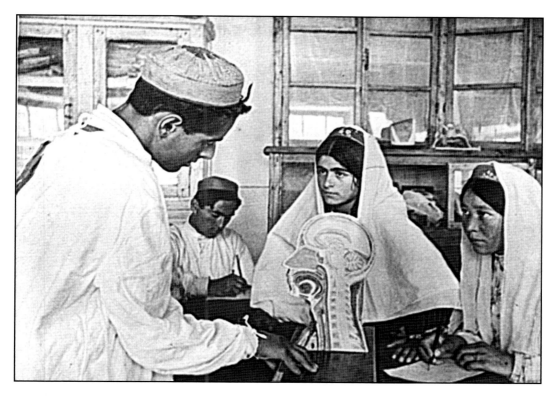

Ethnic Tajik nurses take part in a training course in Khorugh, a city in the Kuhistoni Badakhshon region, circa 1938. Although Tajikistan was the poorest republic in the Soviet Union, the Soviet government provided health care and educational opportunities for most citizens.

of Mecca (the *hajj*), as required by their religion. But Muslims continued to meet and practice their religion in secret, despite the Soviet regime's anti-religious policies. By the mid-1970s, thousands of mullahs, or Islamic religious leaders, were operating clandestinely in the Tajik SSR, and groups of young men were meeting secretly to discuss Islamic revival.

During 1979, Tajik Muslims paid attention to unrest in two neighboring countries. First, in January 1979 the shah of Iran was overthrown in a popular uprising, and an Islamic state established under the Ayatollah Khomeini. The new Iranian government was hostile toward the United States, but Khomeini also encouraged Muslims in the Soviet Union to rise up against their rulers. In December 1979, civil unrest in Afghanistan led the Soviet Army to invade the country and install a puppet communist government. One goal of this incursion was to prevent Afghanistan from becoming an Islamic state like Iran. Another may have been to discourage Muslims in Central Asia from attempting to revolt against the Soviet Union.

Many Tajikistanis were not happy about the Soviet invasion. Because Tajikistan and Afghanistan shared a border, the USSR used the Tajik SSR as a staging area for their invasion. Additionally, Tajiks fighting with the Soviet army wound up battling ethnic Tajiks who lived in Afghanistan. The Soviet incursion, which was condemned by the United Nations and most of the world, ultimately proved unsuccessful. For ten years the Soviet Union was involved in a brutal civil war in Afghanistan.

Collapse of the Soviet Union

In 1985, a reformer named Mikhail Gorbachev came to power in the Soviet Union. He gradually instituted new policies of openness toward the United States and the West (*glasnost*), and moved toward restructuring the Soviet government and economy (*perestroika*). During the 1970s and early 1980s, the Soviet economy had stagnated, while involvement in Afghanistan and an arms race with the United States drained the USSR of resources. Gorbachev hoped his reforms would strengthen the state, but the reform movement instead hastened the demise of the USSR. People in the Soviet Union and the neighboring communist states of Eastern Europe were not satisfied with limited freedoms; they wanted more. As the Soviet grip over Eastern Europe weakened, the people of such countries as Poland and Romania threw off communist governments. In November 1989, the Berlin Wall—a poignant Cold War symbol—came down.

In early August 1991, communist hard-liners tried to overthrow Gorbachev's government. The coup failed, but it was clear that the Soviet Union could not survive. In the aftermath the Soviet republics in Central

Asia and elsewhere declared their independence. Uzbekistan and Kyrgyzstan declared their independence from the Soviet Union on August 19, 1991. Tajikistan left the union less than a month later, on September 9, 1991. However, the collapse of the Soviet Union affected Tajikistan probably more than any of the other Central Asian republics. It was the only one of the five republics to explode into civil war.

Even after the collapse of the USSR, there was a faction in Tajikistan that wanted to maintain a Soviet-style government in Tajikistan. In the chaos that followed Tajikistan's declaration of independence, a communist hard-liner named Rahmon Nabiev was elected president in November 1991. Outside observers considered the election unfair because the communists controlled the media and did not give Nabiev's opponent an opportunity to campaign; it was also marred by widespread allegations of voter fraud.

Several parties soon emerged to challenge Nabiev and the communists, who were resistant to political and economic reforms. One was the Islamic Renaissance Party (IRP), the first legally recognized opposition party of its kind in Central Asia. Another was the Rastokhez ("rebirth") movement, which was led by Tajik nationalists seeking to bring back traditional language and culture. Other active parties included the Democratic Party of Tajikistan (DPT) and La'li Badakhshon.

Leaders of Tajikistan and the other former Soviet republics of Central Asia met in Turkmenistan during December 1991, at an assembly called a *maljis*, to discuss their new independence. A week later, they joined with the leaders of Russia and the other former Soviet republics to found the Commonwealth of Independent States (CIS).

Civil War in Tajikistan

Forces opposed to the Nabiev government—particularly Pamiris who sought to have Kuhistoni Badakhshon elevated to the status of an autonomous republic within Tajikistan—demonstrated in Dushanbe in the spring of 1992. The protestors, whose numbers reached an estimated 100,000, included members of the IRP, Rastokhez, the DPT, La'li Badakhshon, and other groups who sought Nabiev's resignation. They had many complaints. Nabiev had arrested the mayor of Dushanbe, who although a communist had been willing to cooperate with reformers. Many people also felt that restrictions on the press and a crackdown on several prominent reformers showed that Nabiev intended to maintain a Soviet-style authoritarian regime in Tajikistan.

The pro-democracy protests prompted counter-demonstrations from communist supporters in April 1992, and Nabiev distributed weapons to his supporters. In early May government troops fired on the opposition demonstrators in Dushanbe, killing several people. Violence broke out, and the Russian army had to enter the country to restore order. To stabilize the country Nabiev agreed to work with his opponents in a coalition government that would share power. However, this so-called Government of National Reconciliation (GNR) was unsuccessful, primarily because Nabiev and his allies—members of the ruling elite who remained from the Soviet era—did their best to ensure that no power would actually be shared with their reformist opponents.

Most of the pro-government demonstrators turned in their weapons to the Russian military, but one group returned with their arms to their homes in the Kulob province. This became the nucleus of what would become known as the Popular Front militia. Over the summer, the Popular Front began attacking people who did not belong to their faction. As an armed opposition to the pro-government Popular Front began to coalesce

Tajik refugees wait near trucks at the Pianche border post in December 1992. During the civil war, thousands of Muslims who opposed the Rahmonov government fled across the border to Afghanistan.

among Islamist and nationalist parties, it became known as the United Tajik Opposition.

In September 1992, Nabiev was forced to resign. Akbarsho Iskandarov, the speaker of the parliament (known as the Supreme Soviet), became acting president. However, he was unable to end the violence, which continued through the fall and was particularly bloody in Hisor and Qurghonteppa.

Imomali Rahmonov was a minor Communist Party official, who rose from being the director of a collective cotton farm to being elected head of Tajikistan's Supreme Soviet in a matter of months during 1992. Although Rahmonov won reelection in 1997 with 97 percent of the vote, international observers criticized the election process as being stacked in his favor. In 2003, Rahmonov and his supporters pushed through a constitutional change that would allow him to remain in power until 2020.

In November 1992 the Iskandarov government resigned. At a session of the Supreme Soviet, some members attempted to reinstate Nabiev as president, but he declined. Instead, a new government was formed. The office of president was abolished, and Imomali Rahmonov, as the elected head of Tajikistan's Supreme Soviet, became the new leader of the government.

With the support of soldiers from Russia and Uzbekistan, Rahmonov's forces gained control over Tajikistan. Once firmly in power, Rahmonov's government began a campaign of repression of the opposition parties. The IRP and other dissenting groups were banned, and their leaders charged with crimes against the state. Nearly all opposition leaders left the country. Many of those who remained were arrested and executed.

The worst of the fighting ended in January 1993, but sporadic violence continued over the next few years, particularly along the Tajikistan-Afghanistan border, where rebel groups that had fled Tajikistan continued to launch attacks, mostly against the Russian soldiers who were guarding the border.

The office of president was reinstated in June 1994 and Rahmonov was elected to that office. Voters also elected a new parliament and a new constitution. However, observers of the election said that the vote was rigged, and that the process had not met Western standards for a "free and fair" election.

Under pressure from Russia, Iran, and neighboring states, the United Nations sponsored peace negotiations in Tajikistan that were ultimately successful. In 1997, a peace agreement was finalized. As part of the agreement, the government—which, although in the hands of Rahmonov's People's Democratic Party, functions much like the old communist government—promised to share power with the opposition and the IRP was legalized.

Approximately 60,000 people were killed in Tajikistan's civil war, and possibly ten times that number were displaced by the fighting. Some 200,000 people fled the country as refugees. The estimated total monetary cost of the war was $7 billion.

Although the peace has held, the nation's calm is tenuous. Violent regional clashes occur sporadically. The capital, Dushanbe, is plagued by organized crime. Armed bandits make travel in the mountains around Tajikistan's border with Kyrgyzstan dangerous. Illegal drug trafficking from Afghanistan is rampant. Tajikistan remains dependent on Russia, as well as on such new allies as the United States, to help it continue to function as an independent nation.

Russian border guards display 2,200 pounds (1,000 kg) of heroin, valued at over $300 million, seized near the border of Tajikistan and Afghanistan in 2004. The poverty of most Tajiks makes the lucrative cultivation of opium poppies and processing of heroin an attractive source of income, although in recent years the government of Tajikistan has cracked down on drug smugglers.

Politics, Religion, and the Economy

A casual observer might think that as an independent country, Tajikistan has developed a democratic government. After all, the people elect Tajikistan's president and members of one of the two houses in its legislature. The truth, however, is that a handful of political elites, many of whom are holdovers from the Soviet era, maintain tight control over the government. Independent observers, including the U.S. Department of State, have found that elections in the country are not fair, and that Tajikistan's government is more **authoritarian** than democratic. The political party of President Rahmonov, the People's Democratic Party of Tajikistan, dominates both legislative houses. That gives him near-total control over legislation. Some opposition parties are legal, but their members complain that they are watched and, at times, jailed. Tajikistan's government claims that it permits freedom of the press, but journalists say they are threatened if they write stories critical of the government. In addition, the government owns most of the mass media, ensuring that unfavorable stories are quashed. A 2002 report on human rights practices in Tajikistan by the U.S. State Department contends that "members of government security forces and government-aligned militias committed serious human rights abuses," including arbitrary arrests, torture, and infringement on citizens' right to privacy.

The Government

In November 1994, the people of Tajikistan approved a new constitution, which was written after the worst of the fighting in Tajikistan's civil war ended in 1993. Some parts of the constitution were amended during the 1997 peace agreement that officially ended the civil war. The changes were intended to make the government more democratic, but this has not yet happened.

In Tajikistan's government, the president has a great deal of power. President Rahmonov maintains tight control over the legislature, through the dominant People's Democratic Party, and over the judiciary, because he appoints judges. The president also appoints ministers, who oversee the operations of different areas of government, such as finance, foreign relations, and defense. Although the Supreme Assembly (called the Majlisi Oli) must approve the 18 ministers nominated by the president, this has been merely a rubber-stamp. There are few checks on the president's power; it is virtually impossible to impeach him, for example.

Rahmonov was elected to a seven-year term as president in 1999 with 96 percent of the vote, although international observers reported numerous election irregularities. The constitution prohibited Rahmonov from running for another term in 2006, but in June 2003 voters approved a constitutional change, through a referendum, that allows the president to serve two seven-year terms, not including current or prior terms. Supporters of the measure argued that the referendum brought Tajikistan's constitution in line with many other countries, including the United States, where presidents are

Tajikstan's Prime Minister Akil Akilov (right) meets Chinese Premier Wen Jiabao in Beijing. The prime minister and other top government officials in Tajikistan are appointed by the president.

allowed two terms. But opposition parties complained bitterly, because it would allow Rahmonov to remain in power until 2020. A report by researchers at the Center for International Development and Conflict Management (CIDCM) at the University of Maryland called it "a troubling sign for the future of democratic institutions in Tajikistan."

Tajikistan's legislature, the Supreme Assembly, is comprised of two parts: a lower chamber, the 63-member Majlisi Namoyandagon, or Assembly of Representatives, and an upper chamber, the 33-member Majlisi Milli, or National Assembly. Members of the Majlisi Namoyandagon are elected by voters to five-year terms. Terms in the Majlisi Milli are also for five years, but 25 of its 33 members are selected by local officials. The rest are appointed by the president. The lower house meets regularly, while the upper house meets less frequently, but at least twice a year.

One of the conditions of the 1997 peace agreement was that 30 percent of government and judicial posts would be allocated to members of the opposition. However, the People's Democratic Party retains a permanent legislative majority. After the 2000 election for the Majlisi Namoyandagon, the PDP held 65 percent of the seats, followed by the Communist Party (20 percent).

Tajikistan is the only country in Central Asia in which a religiously affiliated party holds any legislative seats. The Islamic Renaissance Party has the third-largest representation in the Majlisi Namoyandagon, with 7.5 percent of the seats. Several other political parties operate in the country, including the Socialist Party, which is typically allied with government forces, and the Democratic Party, which is a secular party. Other parties have been banned for their ties to various religious or opposition groups. When the government bans a political party, it sometimes accuses the party of involvement in terrorist acts. Linking dissident parties to terrorism, even without proof, is an effective way for the government to repress political opponents while deflecting criticism for this repression.

An elderly Tajik man casts his ballot during the parliamentary election in Dushanbe, February 2000. The president's party, the People's Democratic Party of Tajikistan (PDPT), currently controls a majority of both houses in the legislature.

Members of minority parties that have not fared well in elections argue that the contests do not give everyone an even chance. The U.S. State Department agreed in a report that characterized the parliamentary elections as "neither free nor fair." The CIDCM went further, saying that elections in Tajikistan are more of a coronation than a contest. "President Rahmonov, although subject to an election procedure, has gained and retained office through private negotiations with a relatively small cadre of established political elites," the organization reported in its *Polity IV Country Report 2002.* "Elections in Tajikistan remain simply a legitimizing ritual."

Religion in Tajikistan

Approximately 90 percent of Tajikistanis follow Islam, one of the world's major monotheistic religions. Muslims believe in a single God, known in Arabic as Allah ("father"). They believe Allah is the same God that Jews and Christians worship. The word *Islam* is derived from the Arabic verb *aslama*, which means "to submit"; Muslims believe that by obeying the tenets of their religion they are submitting to Allah's requirements for their lives, and that their devotion to God will result in peace, justice, and equality.

The tenets of Islam were set forth by the Prophet Muhammad, who was born on the Arabian Peninsula around A.D. 570. When Muhammad was about 40 years old, he was visited by the Angel Gabriel, who told him that there is only one God and that Muhammad was to be His messenger. Over the next 22 years, Muhammad received a number of revelations from Allah. These teachings were ultimately recorded in the **Qur'an**, the holy scriptures upon which Islam is based. Around the year 613 Muhammad began to teach others the revelations he received from Allah. Although he and his followers initially faced persecution and hardship, his message was gradually accepted. By the time of his death in 632 he had united many of the Arab tribes under the banner of Islam.

After Muhammad's death, the Muslims became divided over the issue of who would succeed the Prophet as their leader on earth. A majority of Muslims wanted the leader to be chosen because of his faith and personal character, but a smaller group wanted the leader to come from Muhammad's immediate family. The disagreement over the succession lasted for generations, and caused several wars within the Muslim community. Ultimately, the Muslims split into two major groups, Sunni and Shiite Muslims. The Sunni make up the largest group of Muslims today—more than 80 percent of the worldwide Muslim population of approximately 1.25 billion. Sunni teachings are sometimes known as "orthodox" Islam. The Shiites, who make up about 14 percent of the global Muslim population, hold some different beliefs about the importance of prayer leaders and the role of saints in religious life. (Followers of various smaller sects make up the rest of the global Islamic population.)

Despite their differences, both Sunni and Shiite Muslims share five basic beliefs, known as the five pillars of Islam. The first of these is a profession of faith (in Arabic, *shahada*), in which Muslims must declare, "There is no god but Allah, and Muhammad is His messenger." The second is prayer (*salat*), as Muslims are required to say certain prayers at five specific times of the day. The third pillar involves charity (*zakat*), as all Muslims must give to the poor or needy. Fourth is the duty to fast (*sawm*), the requirement that Muslims must abstain from eating, drinking, and certain other activities in the daytime hours during the month of **Ramadan**, the ninth month of the Islamic lunar calendar. Finally, all Muslims are expected to make a ritual pilgrimage (*hajj*) to the holy city of Mecca at some time during their lifetime, if they are physically and financially able to do so.

Sunni Islam spread into Central Asia more than 1,200 years ago. Today, about 85 percent of Tajikistanis are Sunni Muslims, and about 5 percent are Shiites. Some of those considered Shiites are actually members of an even smaller sect, the Ismailis, which broke away from the mainstream of Shia Islam in the tenth century. Most Ismailis in Tajikistan live in remote areas of the Pamir region.

During the 1920s and 1930s the Soviet government tried to end the role of religion in people's lives, but these efforts were largely unsuccessful. After Germany invaded the Soviet Union in 1941, Stalin moderated his anti-religion policies to gain support for the defense of the U.S.S.R. Soviet officials created the Muslim Board of Central Asia in 1943 to oversee religious matters. However, once the war was won Soviet officials again sought to eradicate the practice of Islam. They tried to link it with backwardness, superstition, and prejudice. But these efforts failed and most Muslims remained committed to their religion. During the 1980s, Soviet leader Mikhail Gorbachev's more open policies led to an increase in religious instruction in Tajikistan, the opening of new mosques, and a

Muslims pray at a mosque in Dushanbe. About 90 percent of Tajikistan's population follows Islam; most Tajik Muslims adhere to the Sunni branch of the faith.

rise in the popularity of religious observances. Participation in religion has been much greater since the fall of the Soviet Union.

Observers have noted that there is a difference in the degree to which Muslims in Tajikistan and other countries of Central Asia adhere to the rules of Islam. Tajikistanis are fairly open to other ideas, and do not practice the faith as strictly as do Muslims in countries such as Saudi Arabia or Iran. Islam appears to be as much a part of Tajikistan's cultural heritage as a religion.

About 10 percent of Tajikistan's population does not follow Islam. Most of these people are Christians, with the Russian Orthodox Church being the largest denomination. The Russian Orthodox Church developed from the Eastern Orthodox Church in the tenth century. Other Christian denominations also have followers, and there is a small Jewish community within Tajikistan as well.

Tajikistan's constitution provides for freedom of religion. However, the law requires religious communities to register with the State Committee on Religious Affairs, so there is some regulation of religions. State officials have plenty of leeway to deny registration.

The Government and Religion

Although most Tajiks are Muslim, Rahmonov and other political leaders do not want to see the establishment of a religious state, such as the one that exists in Iran. Today Tajikistan is a secular, not an Islamic, state.

The government has used the threat of religious extremism to justify tightening its own grip on society. For example, in 2001 the government claimed that members of the Taliban militia, which ruled Afghanistan according to strict Islamic law and harbored the terrorist Osama bin Laden, were moving toward the Afghan-Tajik border. Tajikistan's government used this report as justification for cracking down on those it labled Muslim radicals within Tajikistan. In 2002, Rahmonov charged that the IRP was spreading extremist views. Then officials began testing imams (Islamic spiritual leaders) on secular law in the country. Ten imams were barred from preaching because of the tests. Later that year Rahmonov ordered the closure of dozens of mosques in the Isfara District in northern Tajikistan, near the border with Uzbekistan and Kyrgyzstan. Government officials said they closed the mosques because the district had too many of them and not all were registered with the state, as the law required. The government also removed a fifth of the district's imams, saying they had become involved in politics. Officials in the IRP complained that these actions were an attempt by Rahmonov to gain more political control over a region that is more religiously conservative and where the IRP won by large majorities in the 2000 parliamentary elections.

Government officials also have been keeping a close eye on Hizb ut-Tahrir, a radical underground Islamic organization, and have imprisoned some of its members for subversion. The group has been targeted because of its links with an organization of the same name in Uzbekistan that has called for the creation of a Muslim caliphate—a land ruled by the successor of the Muslim prophet Muhammad—in that country. The government of Uzbekistan considers the group an extremist organization and has accused its members of acting against the constitution.

Tajikistan, like the governments of other Central Asian states, actively promotes fear of Islamist groups like Hizb ut-Tahrir as a way to justify repression. In 2002, 142 members of Hizb ut-Tahrir were jailed in

Pakistani supporters of Hizb ut-Tahrir protest during a 2004 visit by President Rahmonov to Lahore, demanding the release of more than 100 member of the organization imprisoned in Tajikstan.

Tajikistan. However, in some cases people arrested for being Hizb ut-Tahrir activists may not have actually been members, and some of the acts of violence for which the organization has been blamed by the regime may have been committed by common criminals or other political groups.

Although the government crackdown on Islam may be unfair, religious extremism is a potential problem in Central Asia. In the summers of 1999 and 2000, the Islamic Movement of Uzbekistan, which the United States recognizes as a terrorist organization, launched campaigns against the government of Uzbekistan from inside Tajikistan. The IMU is a group of militant Muslims who propose to overthrow the current government in Uzbekistan and create an Islamic state there. Among its members are men who fought in Tajikistan's civil war.

A Weak Economy

One thing that could give Islamic militants a stronger position in Tajikistan is the relatively poor state of the country's economy. Tajikistan is still trying to recover from its five-year civil war. By one measure—the yearly amount of income per person—Tajikistan is among the 20 poorest countries in the world. The average annual income is the equivalent of about $330 a year, but many people earn much less than that. In 2003, one international aid organization estimated the average monthly salary at $7, and reported that 40 percent of Tajikistan's population was unemployed.

Tajikistan's economy is heavily dependent on just a few major exports, particularly cotton and aluminum. This leaves the economy very sensitive to even small disturbances in the prices of these commodities. Today, the most thriving "business" is the drug trade, with smugglers moving truck-loads of heroin from Afghanistan through Tajikistan into Russia and Europe. Russian soldiers are ostensibly in the country to help Tajik officials stop as much of the trafficking as possible, although over the years,

The Economy of Tajikistan

Gross domestic product (GDP*): $1.64 billion

GDP per capita: $252

Inflation: 7 percent

Natural resources: hydropower, some petroleum, uranium, mercury, brown coal, lead, zinc, antimony, tungsten, silver, gold

Agriculture (31 percent of GDP): cotton, grain, fruits, grapes, vegetables; cattle, sheep, goats

Industry (29 percent of GDP): aluminum, zinc, lead, chemicals and fertilizers, cement, vegetable oil, metal-cutting machine tools, refrigerators and freezers

Services (40 percent of GDP): Government, banking, tourism, other

Foreign trade:
  Imports—$890 million: electricity, petroleum products, aluminum oxide, machinery and equipment, foodstuffs
  Exports—$750 million: aluminum, electricity, cotton, fruits, vegetable oil, textiles

Currency exchange rate: 2.76 Tajikistan somoni = $1 US (2004).

* GDP or gross domestic product is the total value of goods and services produced in a country annually.

All figures are 2003 estimates unless otherwise noted.

Sources: U.S. State Department; CIA World Factbook 2004.

some Russian border guards have been arrested on drug smuggling charges.

There is little doubt Tajikistan is in worse shape financially than it was before the Soviet Union collapsed in 1991. Tajikistan found it difficult to operate an independent economy without the support of the Soviet Union, which provided 40 percent of the country's annual budget revenue. During the 1992–97 civil war, agricultural production dropped precipitously; also, because of the war private investors avoided Tajikistan, focusing instead on development in the other former Soviet republics.

Tajikistan's economy is based on agriculture, even though much of the land is unsuitable for growing crops. During the early part of the Soviet era, farms had been mechanized and irrigation systems had been constructed to increase the production of cotton. But by the 1990s, the irrigation infrastructure and much of the farm equipment had aged and were breaking down. When a drought hit the region in 2000 and 2001, farmers in Tajikistan could not even grow enough to feed their own countrymen, much less extra crops for export.

Even when Tajikistan produces a surplus of goods for export, the country is at a disadvantage because it has no access to major bodies of water.

Women pick cotton in a field in northern Tajikstan. Cotton is the main cash crop, and requires most of the country's supplies of irrigated water.

Tajikistan must ship its goods through neighboring countries, but each time a border is crossed taxes and fees are added to the cost of those goods. To ease this burden the United Nations included Tajikistan in a special program that assists developing countries that are landlocked.

During the Soviet era, all businesses and industries were owned by the state. After the breakup of the Soviet Union in 1991, Russia and the other Central Asian republics moved to privatize industries, selling ownership to private individuals or corporations. This measure was intended to stimulate investment in the economies of those countries. Tajikistan, however, has lagged behind in privatizing state-run businesses. By 2004, the State Property Committee still had not completed its work.

In any case, privatization is not a cure for all economic ills, as corruption in the system is a major issue. In many Central Asian countries, government officials granted control over lucrative businesses to friends

During the Soviet era, the flag of the Tajik SSR was red with two horizontal stripes of white (symbolizing cotton production) and green (representing other agriculture). The flag of Tajikistan (pictured above) incorporates the same three colors, but its current design is similar to the flag of Iran, a country with which the Tajiks share cultural and linguistic ties.

or family members for less than market prices. Such deals, which enrich a few people at the expense of the majority, have also been a problem in Tajikistan.

The country also had trouble establishing a stable monetary system. After declaring independence, Tajikistan continued to use the Russian ruble for a time, but a shortage forced it to create its own currency, the Tajikistani ruble. The value of the Tajikistani ruble dropped precipitously, though, so that by October 2000 it took 2,400 Tajikistani rubles to equal $1. By the end of that month, Tajikistan changed its currency again, this time to the *somoni*, which was set to equal about $2. Since then the currency has been more stable.

The economic picture in the country is not entirely grim. Tajikistan has one of the world's largest aluminum processing facilities, and the country exports more than $300 million worth of aluminum annually. This plant, however, needs to be modernized and at present the country does not have the money for the necessary upgrades. In addition, Tajikistan must import the essential raw materials from which to make aluminum.

The country is receiving help from several international organizations. Tajikistan has borrowed from the International Development Association of the World Bank to improve infrastructure in rural areas, privatize businesses that had been government-owned during Soviet rule, and increase the quality of social services. Additionally, it is part of the CIS 7 Initiative, an international effort to bring economic growth to, and reduce poverty in, the seven lowest-income members of the Commonwealth of Independent States.

With additional aid flowing in the early years of the new millennium, some economic indicators have improved. The statistical office of the Commonwealth of Independent States reported that Tajikistan's **gross domestic product** rose 10.2 percent in 2003. The nation's foreign debt, however, rose 1.5 percent that year to more than $1 billion.

An intricately carved statue of a woman stands in a courtyard in Tajikistan. The primary cultural influences on Tajik society are Russian and Persian.

5

The People

$\mathcal{U}$nlike the people who live in the other former Soviet republics in Central Asia, who are ethnically Turkic, the Tajiks are descended from Persian-speaking Iranian peoples. But Tajiks are not the only people living in Tajikistan. Because of the way the Soviet Union carved Central Asia into republics in the 1920s, many Tajiks were placed in other countries and people of other heritages wound up in Tajikistan.

Ethnic Tajiks comprise about two-thirds of their country's population, and they live throughout the country. Uzbeks are the second-largest ethnic group in Tajikistan, making up about one-quarter of the total population. They live primarily in the north, west, and southwest. The third largest ethnic group is the Russians, who make up 3.5 percent. At one time there were many more Russians in Tajikistan. The Soviet government encouraged Russians to immigrate to Tajikistan, offering high-paying management jobs and positions for skilled laborers. As a result Russians dominated major cities like Dushanbe. However, their numbers have dwindled since 1991—it is estimated that more than 70 percent of the Russian and Ukrainian population have left the country since Tajikistan declared its independence.

The rest of the people are Tartars, Ukrainians, Jews, and people from neighboring countries—the Kyrgyz, Turkmen, and Kazakhs. Of those, Kyrgyz are the largest group, living primarily near the Chinese border and the north-central border between Kyrgyzstan and Tajikistan.

Many people who are ethnic Tajiks do not live in Tajikistan. Approximately 3.5 million ethnic Tajiks live in neighboring Afghanistan, where they make up about a quarter of that country's population. Tajiks have been part of Afghanistan's population for centuries, although some Tajikistanis fled there during Tajikistan's civil war. The Northern Alliance, which fought against the Taliban, included many ethnic Tajiks from Afghanistan, such as Ahmad Shah Massoud, an Alliance leader who was assassinated in September 2001.

Many ethnic Tajiks also live in Uzbekistan, because of the way the Soviet government drew the border between the two republics. The Tajik population of Uzbekistan is currently estimated at about one million. However, because of decades of assimilation and pressure on people to describe themselves as Uzbek on official documents, no one really knows how many Tajiks live in Uzbekistan today.

Language

Nearly all people living in Tajikistan speak Tajik, which is a Persian language and the official language of the state. However, during the Soviet era the official language was Russian, and today Russian is still used extensively in government, particularly in international dealings. This has

The People of Tajikistan

Population: 7,011,556
Ethnic Groups: Tajik 64.9%, Uzbek 25%, Russian 3.5%
    (declining because of emigration), other 6.6%
Age structure:
    0-14 years: 39%
    15-64 years: 56%
    65 years and over: 5%
Population growth rate: 2.14%
Birth rate: 32.63 births per 1,000 population
Death rate: 8.42 deaths per 1,000 population
Infant mortality rate: 112.1 deaths per 1,000 live births
Life expectancy:
    Overall: 64.47 years
    Male: 61.53 years
    Female: 67.55 years
Fertility rate: 4.11 children born per woman
Literacy: 99.4%

All figures are 2003 estimates.
Source: CIA World Factbook 2004

been a source of embarassment for Tajik officials. School lessons are taught in Tajik, but in 2003 President Rahmonov ordered that Russian be taught again as well.

The way in which Tajik is written has changed over time. Before 1928, the Perso-Arabic script was used. From 1928 through 1940, Tajik was written with the Latin alphabet. After that time, the language was written with a modified version of the **Cyrillic** alphabet, which is also used to write the Russian language. Although after independence Tajikistan's government tried to reintroduce use of the Latin alphabet, the country continues to rely on the Cyrillic alphabet today.

Some Tajiks are trilingual, speaking a Turkic language like Uzbek or another Persian dialect in addition to Tajik and Russian. In addition, the constitution gives people who don't speak Tajik the right to speak their native language. For instance, those living in the Pamirs speak several different dialects. Among the languages spoken in the remote mountain region are Wakhi, Yazgulom, and Shughni. Other languages spoken by just a few people include Yaghnobi and Parya.

Education in Tajikistan

Despite the many problems that followed Tajikistan's independence, the country's educational system continued to function. According to data from the CIA World Factbook, 99 percent of Tajikistanis age 15 or older can read and write. The high literacy rate is somewhat surprising, given that the condition of the country's school buildings has deteriorated since the end of Soviet rule and there is little money to make repairs. The literacy rate is likely to drop in the future. At the start of the new millennium, fewer than two-thirds of the school-aged children in Tajikistan were enrolled in school.

Many schools are overcrowded and paper and other equipment are in short supply. Preschools do exist, but few parents send their children to them. Typically children begin school at age seven. Elementary school lasts for nine years, followed by two or three years in secondary school. Some students choose a vocational school, which combines job training with academics. Few go on for postsecondary education.

The nation's major institute of higher education is Tajikistan University in Dushanbe, but there are several other colleges. In 1999, the Science and Education Development Association was formed by the eight largest postsecondary schools. Its mission is to ensure that college students in Tajikistan get a world-class education by promoting research and bringing technology like the Internet to the schools.

As it tries to improve schooling for younger children, Tajikistan in 2003 welcomed $20 million in loans through the World Bank to support elementary education projects.

Everyday Life

Most people in Tajikistan—70 percent—live in rural villages rather than in the cities. Unlike other developing countries, the percentage of the population living outside cities has been increasing, rather than dropping. That is due at least in part to the large number of Russians and other urban-dwelling foreigners who have left the country.

City dwellers often wear Western-style clothing. For men, that means a shirt and slacks, or a suit with a tie for business dress. Men may be clean-shaven. Women may wear dresses without any head covering, or the more traditional may wear a scarf or kerchief covering their hair and neck.

Tajik women stand outside their modest home in the village of Asht. Most of Tajikistan's population lives in rural villages.

Those living in rural areas often wear more traditional clothes. For men, that means a quilted coat called a *tapan* tied with a sash and, frequently, an elaborately decorated turban cap, called a *kolah*, or an embroidered skullcap. Men often have beards or mustaches. For women, traditional clothing means a multi-colored dress, called a *kurta*, which is worn over bright pants with a matching headscarf or shawl. Although in the most conservative Islamic countries—such as Afghanistan under Taliban rule—women wear dark clothing that covers them from head to toe, Tajik women often wear brightly colored clothing (red is particularly popular). Many women wear scarves that cover their hair.

Women are treated with differing degrees of equality, depending on where they live and their family background. A practice called the "bride price" is still common in Tajikistan. A man will pay a woman's father money, clothing, or animals to be able to marry her. After marriage, the couple lives with his family. In some cases, three generations of a family—parents, their unmarried children and their married sons with their wives and children—live together in the same house. The eldest man is considered the head of a household. When he dies, his inheritance is passed down through his sons, not his daughters.

But Tajikistani women do have more freedom to move around in society and to work than they do in stricter Muslim countries. Many women have to work because so many men migrate to wealthier countries like Russia to work for a few months each year to make enough money to support their families. One estimate is that at least one member of every four families in Tajikistan seeks employment in another country. Between 2000 and 2003, some 630,000 Tajiks went abroad to work. The women who are left behind in the rural villages may sell milk and cheese, vegetables, or chickens to help make ends meet.

The main staple in a Tajik family's diet is flatbread, or *non*, made out of wheat flour, dried peas, and mulberries. *Osh*, a combination of rice, mutton,

A young Tajik woman, wearing a scarf, walks with other pedestrians through the main bazaar in Isfara, a town near the borders with Kyrgyzstan and Uzbekistan.

and vegetables, is a common dinner meal. Grapes, dried fruits, chicken, and yogurt also are staples. People drink green tea with almost every meal.

Men often get together to talk and conduct business at choikhonas (chaikhanas), or teahouses. These may be ornate buildings with detailed woodcarvings or simply a spot outdoors with some mats tossed about. The choikhonas may also serve sweets, kabobs, and rice. Sometimes music is featured.

Population explosion

Tajikistan has a high birth rate—almost 33 births per 1,000 people, compared with 14 per 1,000 in the United States. It is estimated that each

Residents line up to buy bread in one of Tajikistan's cities. The country is one of the poorest nations in the world.

woman gives birth to slightly more than four children, on average, during her lifetime. As a result, the country's population increased by 14 percent between 1990 and 2000. The age distribution of Tajiks is uneven: half the people are under age 20, and a third are under age 10.

One reason for the high birth rate is that conservative Islamic tradition encourages large families. Additionally, the former Soviet system rewarded women who had more than four children with tax breaks, child benefits, and pensions. But the large number of babies is exacerbating the country's poverty—more children are born into poor rural families than to comparatively wealthier city dwellers. And it also aggravated the food crisis brought on by the drought of 2000–01, which was the worst in 75 years.

To try to decrease family size, Tajikistan's parliament in 2002 passed legislation that encourages women to practice birth control. However, few women have access to birth-control pills or other devices.

Just as Tajikistan has a high birth rate, it also has a high infant mortality rate. More than 11 percent of children born in Tajikistan die in infancy. By contrast, the infant death rate in the United States is less than .007 percent (7 deaths in 1,000 births).

Poverty, inadequate nutrition for mothers and infants, and a lack of clean drinking water in some places due to environmental pollution are some of the causes of Tajikistan's high infant mortality rate. Another reason may be the deterioration of the health care system, as the infant mortality rate has been on the rise since the late 1980s.

Health Care

During the Soviet era, people had access to free health care. In some areas the medical system was adequate, but in other areas there were fewer facilities, and the ones that were available had second-rate equipment, inadequate sanitation, and poor quality health-care personnel.

By the mid-1990s it was estimated that 80 percent of the health care facilities in Tajikistan were substandard—many lacking central heat and running water. It became hard for the average person to get some medications.

Surprisingly, the situation was better in the most remote region—Kuhistoni Badakhshon, which includes the Pamir Mountains. Each village there had at least a medical aid station and there was a hospital for

Women were encouraged to have large families when Tajikistan was part of the Soviet Union. The government bestowed the award "Hero Mother Order" on some 10,000 women who had 10 children or more.

every *jamoat*, or group of villages. Even today there are nearly 10 beds for every 100 residents of the region, which is comparable to the ratio found in many Western countries.

Many doctors and other health care professionals—a large number of them Russian, Ukrainian, and Jewish—left the country during the civil war. By 1994, there was only one doctor for every 450 people, the worst proportion of any of the former Soviet republics. The situation has improved slightly since then, but many more trained health-care professionals are needed.

Two women scoop dirty water from the bottom of a dried-up pool in the village of Gazantarak, northern Tajikistan. Although the villagers believe that the water causes health problems, they have no alternative source of clean drinking water.

Festivals and Celebrations

The Tajiks are a friendly people who love to celebrate and socialize. When strangers meet, they greet one another by putting their thumbs together, a way of offering their assistance. To express respect for another person, a man will bow with his right hand on his chest, while a woman bows with both hands on hers.

Travelers, especially in rural areas like the Pamirs, are welcomed with open doors and tables of food. Guests often are served bread, hot tea with goat's milk (called *sher chay*), and yogurt made from goat's milk. Those who arrive during a special celebration, including a wedding, are invited to join in—the arrival of a stranger at a wedding is considered good luck and it would be considered disrespectful for the guest to refuse to participate.

An entire village might attend the wedding feast for two of its members. To profess their commitment to each other, the bride and groom eat from the same bowl and drink from the same cup. They also exchange rings. Drums are played and a wedding song is sung. Playing a long horn is often part of a wedding or other joyful celebration in Tajikistan, such as a birth or a homecoming.

There are other rituals to celebrate births as well. When a boy is born, three shots are fired or three cheers shouted loudly to wish him health and a good life. For newborn girls, a broom is placed under the baby's pillow so she will become a good housewife.

Tajiks celebrate many special holidays. One unique celebration called Navruz is held during the vernal equinox—the first day of spring. Known as the Persian New Year, the celebration typically lasts from March 20 to 22 and features bonfires, poetry readings, music, games, and art. Men eat *halim*, a traditional beef dish, while women eat *sumalak*, a concoction that includes wheat. People also partake of wine, milk, sweets and sherbet.

In Tajikistan, as in other Muslim countries, tea symbolizes hospitality and friendship, and teahouses are a popular meeting spot for Tajik men.

Navruz is one of several public holidays observed in Tajikistan. The others include New Year's Day (January 1), International Women's Day (March 8), International Day of Solidarity (May 1), Victory Day (May 9), the Day of National Unity (June 27), Independence Day (September 9), and Constitution Day (November 6).

Two Islamic holy days also have been declared state holidays. Because the Muslim lunar calendar differs from the 365-day solar calendar, these festivals fall on different dates each year. One of those occurs at the end of Ramadan, the month in which Muslims fast from sunrise to sunset. It is called Eid al-Fitr or Eid i-Ramazon. It is a two- or three-day celebration that includes large meals enjoyed with families and also involves making donations to the poor. The other Islamic holy celebration is known as Eid al-Adha or Eid i-Qurbon, the Feast of Sacrifice. Celebrated about 70 days after Ramadan, this festival commemorates the Patriarch Abraham's willingness to sacrifice his son to God. (Allah told him to sacrifice a sheep instead.) As part of the multi-day celebration, an animal is slaughtered and shared with family members and the poor.

Several thousand men travel to Mecca, the birthplace of Islam, each year for the *hajj*, the pilgrimage required of faithful Muslims. The *hajj* takes place during the final month of the Islamic lunar calendar.

Entertainment and the Arts

Sports are popular among men in Tajikistan. One favorite sport is soccer, and the country has a national team that competes in the World Cup.

Men in Tajik villages get together for a fast-paced physical sport called *buskashi* (a rough translation would be "drag the goat"). This is a very physical game played with a goat carcass instead of a ball. Omir Agakhanyantz, who traveled through the Pamirs studying the plants and landforms, was invited to observe a *buskashi* match in one village. "A goat is killed, its head cut off, its skin removed, and the carcass is thrown into a ring," he wrote. "The horsemen dash into the ring from all directions. One has to seize the carcass while riding one's horse, gallop with it to the end of the field and throw it over the finish line . . . During the game, one can grab the carcass from another player, force him out of his saddle and the like. There are few restrictive rules and sometimes none at all. The game threatens the players with injury or worse."

Tajikistan also is known for calmer pursuits: its arts and crafts. For instance, the Pamiri handcraft decorative embroidered cloths, called *suzanis*, and brightly colored knitted socks and gloves.

Tajik artwork is a mixed bag of influences from the numerous civilizations that conquered the region over time—including Sogdian, Arab, Greek, and Buddhist. These can be seen in jewelry, pottery, and silverware. Muslim art is not supposed to show living creatures—human or animal—because those images are prohibited by Islam. Instead the art

Tajikstanis play *buskashi*, a Central Asian game in which horsemen try to grab the headless carcass of a goat and ride with it to various points in the field.

that decorates mosques and prayer rugs often features calligraphy, geometric shapes, and flower designs.

Modern Tajik literature had three major figures. The first was Sadriddin Aini, or Ayni (1878–1954). Initially a poet, Aini wrote mostly prose during Soviet rule, when he became a communist. He wrote three major novels about local life and society, including one called *Dokhunda* (*The Mountain Villager*). Abulqosim Lohuti or Abu'l-Qasem, (1887–1957), was an Iranian poet who immigrated to Tajikistan for political reasons. He wrote lyric poetry and realistic verse. "Toju bairaq" or "Taj va bayraq" ("Crown and Banner") was his most famous work. The third major figure was poet Mirzo Tursunzoda (1911–1977). His poems focused on social change and popular political themes in the country.

Tajiks enjoy music and dance as well. Traditional music is very rhythmic, perfect for dancing. Among the instruments played in Bukharan music are a large frame drum called a *doura*. The *tar* and the *tanbur* are stringed instruments in the lute family that are plucked, while the *gidjak* is a long-necked instrument similar to a violin. In dancing to this music, a woman moves her feet quickly forward, backward, and in circles, and waves her arms above her head or at shoulder height. The dancers wear brightly colored costumes and jeweled headdresses.

Another popular form of folk music is *Sozanda*. It features women singing, accompanied by percussion instruments like the tambourine and the *dabyl* and *dauylpaz*, which are small, handheld drums.

A golden crown tops a monument to Tajik folkloric heroes in Dushanbe, the capital of Tajikistan. Dushanbe is the largest city in Tajikistan.

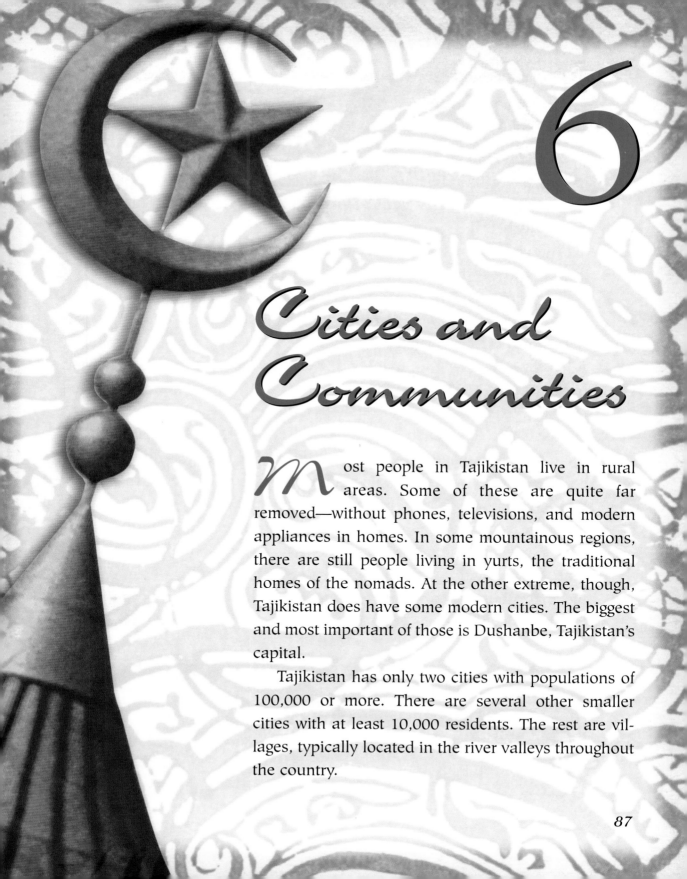

6

Cities and Communities

$\mathcal{M}$ ost people in Tajikistan live in rural areas. Some of these are quite far removed—without phones, televisions, and modern appliances in homes. In some mountainous regions, there are still people living in yurts, the traditional homes of the nomads. At the other extreme, though, Tajikistan does have some modern cities. The biggest and most important of those is Dushanbe, Tajikistan's capital.

Tajikistan has only two cities with populations of 100,000 or more. There are several other smaller cities with at least 10,000 residents. The rest are villages, typically located in the river valleys throughout the country.

Dushanbe

In addition to being the seat of government for Tajikistan, Dushanbe is its largest city. Its population was estimated at 599,900 in 2004. Dushanbe covers 483 square miles (1,250 sq km), and is divided into four administrative districts.

The city was not always such a metropolis. Named after the market that, as early as the 1600s, used to be held there every Monday (the word *dushanbe* means "Monday"), Dushanbe had just 3,000 citizens in 1920. In 1924, after the formation of the U.S.S.R., Dushanbe's official population dropped to 283. Still Soviet officials chose it to be the capital of Tajikistan—renaming it Stalinobod after their leader, Joseph Stalin—and began turning it into an important place in 1930. The name was changed back to Dushanbe in 1961.

Dushanbe is situated in a valley on the southern side of the Hisor Mountain ridge, straddling the Varzob River. The river was an inspiration for the Soviet planners who laid out the city—they left greenways along its banks, which are pleasant places for walking today.

In the 80 or so years that it has been Tajikistan's capital, Dushanbe has been transformed from a town with only 13 streets into a city with more than 270. Rudaki Avenue (known as Lenin Street during Soviet days) is the main thoroughfare. Lining it are numerous monuments and office buildings, including major government facilities. Among these is the home

Dushanbe, Tajikistan's largest city, has the greatest percentage of its population between the ages of 6 and 23 enrolled in schools of any city or village in the country. In Dushanbe, nearly 80 percent of that age group was in school in 2004.

The snow-covered Pamir mountains loom over apartment blocks and small houses in Dushanbe.

of the Supreme Assembly, a bright brick structure with imposing three-story white columns. Under the direction of Soviet architects, many important buildings in the city were constructed in the "empire style" of architecture, with columns, arches, and ornamental patterned porticos.

Industries are located in Dushanbe, particularly those dealing with cotton and silk fabrics. Other businesses make boots, milk, tobacco, leather, and wine. But the end of Soviet rule and the subsequent civil war hurt city industries—only a third of the 90 or so industries in Dushanbe at the start of the 1990s were still operating in 2004.

Dushanbe is also the country's cultural and entertainment capital, with a cinema, circus, eight museums, 30 libraries, and numerous restaurants and teahouses. The stately Theatre of Opera and Ballet, a bright white

A Tajik vendor stands at his stall in the market of Isfara. The population of Isfara is ethnically mixed; although Tajiks are the majority, the town is also home to many Kyrgyz, Uzbeks, Tatars, Russians, and others.

building with tall columns, was constructed in 1939. The city houses the country's only civil aviation airport. The city also is home to more than 200 schools and two dozen colleges.

The city houses two botanical gardens. One, in the northern part of the city, is run by the Academy of Science of Tajikistan. Its area measures 84 acres (34 hectares), and it has 2,190 species of trees and shrubs. It was founded in 1933. The other is an experimental botanical garden operated by Tajik State National University in the western part of the city. It covers 131 acres (53 hectares), and contains 380 species of trees and shrubs. It opened in 1956. Dushanbe also has a zoo, which can be found in the city center, on the Luchob River. According to a joint report by the Ministry for Nature Protection of Tajikistan and the United Nations Environmental Programme, all three of these sites are still suffering financially because of the civil war.

People have lived in the Dushanbe area for thousands of years—the earliest settlement there dates back to the Stone Age. Alexander the Great conquered the area in the fourth century B.C., and it was apparently a stop on the Silk Road. But Dushanbe did not appear on a map until 1875, when it was marked as a fortified city on the Varzob River's steep right bank.

In March 1921, the Red Army entered Dushanbe in search of Sayyid Alim Khan, the last emir of Bukhara, who had fled there to escape the Soviets. In 1925, it became the capital of Tajikistan. Few buildings had survived the Bolshevik fighting, so much rebuilding was necessary. The Soviets embarked on construction projects in 1926, 1938, 1965, and 1983. They had to build structures that were low or specially strengthened because of earthquakes—there were major quakes in 1909, 1911, and 1949.

Most of those who live in the capital are Tajik. Uzbeks and Russians also live there, although the Russian population has declined for numerous reasons since Tajikistan's independence and the start of the civil war. Today, a mayor oversees the government of Dushanbe.

A railway built in 1929, the Termez-Dushanbe, runs through the city, linking it with the country's second largest city, Khujand. Because of the way Tajikistan's boundaries were drawn, trains must pass through Uzbekistan before getting to Khujand.

Khujand

Khujand is the second-largest city in Tajikistan; its 2004 population was estimated at 148,300. During the years of Soviet rule the city was renamed Leninobod (Leninabad) after former Soviet leader Vladimir Lenin, but the city regained its original name in February 1991 as the Soviet Union crumbled.

Khujand is one of the oldest cities in the region, and its recorded history dates back more than 2,000 years. Because it is located in the fertile

Fergana Valley, it has been a key location for centuries and was a major stop along the Silk Road. As such, it was subject to numerous conquests. Alexander the Great stormed through in the fourth century B.C. The Arabs swept into the city in the 700s. In the 1200s, the city was virtually destroyed by Genghis Khan and the Mongols.

Russia took the city in 1866 and turned it into an industrial center. Silk, footwear, and clothing are all manufactured in Khujand today. The city also is a major center of cotton processing. Rare minerals have been found in the region that surrounds Khujand. An early Soviet uranium mine, for example, is located northeast of the city.

Khujand is isolated from the rest of the country, including the capital, which is 205 miles (340 km) away. Like Dushanbe, this city is located on the banks of a river—in this case, the Syr Dar'ya—so it is greener than most of Tajikistan. Khujand still contains many historical monuments, the most famous being the remnants of the city citadel and the mausoleum of Sheykh Muslihiddin, a mystical poet of the middle ages. Khujand is the cultural center of the north and has theaters, museums, teahouses, and a botanical garden. It is also a center of decorative arts.

Smaller Cities

The third-largest city in Tajikistan is Kulob, a cotton-trading town sur- rounded by a region where grain and vegetable farming and livestock breeding predominate. Kulob is located in the Yakhsu River Valley, 125 miles (202 km) southwest of Dushanbe. Most of the approximately 74,000 people who live in this city are ethnic Tajiks.

Kulob's history dates back to the sixth century B.C. The city became part of the Bukharan emirate in 1559. In March 1921, the Soviets took control. In the late 1990s Kulob was a part of a supply route to the Northern Alliance, the group in Afghanistan that opposed the Taliban gov- ernment. Russian soldiers were stationed there as well.

A man walks along rusting railroad tracks toward an abandoned coal mine in the town of Shorab in northwestern Tajikistan. Though during the Soviet era it was a bustling coal mining community, in recent years Shorab has practically become a deserted "ghost town." Other industrial communities in Tajikstan have experienced the same fate.

Kulob was in the news in 2001 following the terrorist attacks on the United States. Because the city is located just 43 miles (70 km) from the border of Afghanistan and it has an international airport, U.S. forces were considering using the city as a base for their campaign in Afghanistan. Although they received permission, the U.S. apparently never staged any operations from the airfield there.

The other large city in Tajikistan is Qurghonteppa, the capital of the southwestern Khatlon province, which is located 57 miles (91 km) outside of Dushanbe. Qurghonteppa's population of about 59,100 is made up mostly of Tajiks and Uzbeks.

Qurghonteppa was an old fortress that became part of the Tajik region of Uzbekistan, before the Soviets created the Republic of Tajikistan in 1924. It is located in the Vakhsh Valley and is the home of many people who were resettled, particularly those from Gharm (Garm), in the north-center of the country, by the Soviets to work the land in the 1930s. The land's agricultural worth was diminished by fighting that broke out there in 1992 as part of the civil war.

Kuhistoni Badakhshon

A region rather than a city, Kuhistoni Badakhshon is one of the most interesting areas of Tajikistan. Measuring almost 25,000 square miles (63,700 sq km), the region—dominated by the Pamir Mountains—comprises nearly half the country's territory. Yet it contains only 3 percent of the population, an estimated 207,000 people.

Formed in 1925, it is the only autonomous province in Tajikistan. One reason why it was given this status was to try to preserve the various ethnicities and languages of the peoples living there. Many of the people living in Kuhistoni Badakhshon are called Pamiris, after the mountains, but they have roots in a number of different groups and speak several different languages. Kuhistoni Badakhshon's *jamoat* system of local governing bodies has been praised by experts as giving people a say in governance and keeping the peace.

Khorugh, the major city of Kuhistoni Badakhshon, is located on the banks of the Ghund River, 7,200 feet (2,200 m) above sea level. The main industries there are shoes, metal goods, building materials, and processed

One statistic in which the rural nature of Kuhistoni Badakhshon is really evident is its maternal mortality rate. In 2001, 111.6 of 100,000 women died giving birth in the province. By comparison, the maternal mortality rate in Dushanbe, Tajikistan's capital, was less than half that figure, at 47.6 deaths per 100,000 women.

foods. It also has a state university and a theater. In 2004, an estimated 32,600 people lived in Khorugh. An old road connects Khorugh with Dushanbe, but because of the harsh weather conditions in winter, portions of the road are only passable during the summer. This region, then, is the most isolated from the rest of the country.

For their livelihoods, people in the region mine for gold, salt, mica, limestone, and coal. They raise yaks, sheep, cattle, and goats, and grow vegetables, beans, and grains. Some farmers, especially those who are Kyrgyz, still live, at least part of the time, in yurts—round, woolen tents resembling small huts.

In the heart of the region is Sarez Lake on the Murghob (Murgab) River. The lake holds 4 cubic miles (17 cubic kilometers) of water. Usoi is the name of the natural dam that keeps the water in the lake. At more than 1,800 feet (550 m) high, it is among the tallest dams in the world, according to the U.N. Office for the Coordination of Humanitarian Affairs, which assessed the stability of the dam in 1999.

Kuhistoni Badakhshon also is home to Tajikistan's first national park, which was designated in 1992. There are acres of virtually undisturbed mountains, forests, deserts, and glaciers. The mountains also are home to the rare Marco Polo sheep, considered among the most valued "trophy animals" in the world.

There are villages in the mountains that are virtually unreachable in the summertime, when warmer weather melts glaciers and the runoff swells rivers. Then, people risk their lives crossing from one bank to another on inflated animal skins.

Russian border guards man an anti-aircraft gun along the Tajikistan-Afghan border, 2001. Russian troops helped restore order, and ensured Rahmonov's government prevailed, during the 1992–97 civil war. Afterward, many Russian soldiers remained in the country, although in 2004 Tajikistan's military began to take over the task of guarding the borders.

7

Foreign Relations

S ince 2001 the United States has seen the value in being involved in Central Asia, and it has sent money and advisors to help prevent Islamist extremists from gaining a foothold in the region. But although in recent years the relationship between Tajikistan and the United States has grown closer, Russia still has the most influence over the former Soviet republic. Russia is Tajikistan's most important trading partner, and plays a key role in defending the country. They are members together in the Commonwealth of Independent States (CIS). Russian President Vladimir Putin has promised more economic and military aid to those countries that support his government, and Tajikistan has been an ardent supporter.

Russian Influence

It has been more than a decade since Tajikistan left the Soviet Union, but Russia remains the country with which Tajikistan has the closest relationship. The two countries are members of the Commonwealth of Independent States (CIS), and both are signatories to numerous pacts and treaties. Russia and Tajikistan together have signed more than 100 cooperative agreements. In May 1992, Tajikistan, Russia, and several other members of the CIS signed the Agreement of Collective Security, which established a common aircraft defense system, as well as a cooperative military structure. The next year Tajikistan and Russia signed the Agreement on Friendship, Cooperation, and Mutual Assistance, probably the most important pact between the two countries. In it, they pledged cooperation in military, political, economic, and scientific endeavors, and Tajikistan agreed to let Russian forces use its airports.

Russian soldiers have been stationed in Tajikistan since the civil war, in which they fought on the side of the hard-line communists. After the war Russia's 201st Motorized Rifle Division continued to guard Tajikistan's border with Afghanistan as well as the Norak hydroelectric plant, which provides energy to much of Central Asia. Russian troops are also working to stem drug trafficking from Afghanistan. However, in June 2004 the task of guarding the border began to be handed over to Tajikistan's Border Guard. Officials from the United States and European Union were part of an assessment team that helped ensure a smooth transition from Russian to Tajikistani guards, and determining what measures were needed to improve border security.

Russia and Tajikistan have a close trade relationship as well. Approximately 20 percent of Tajikistan's exports are sent to Russia, while more than a third of Tajikistan's imports come from Russia. Tajikistan relies heavily on Russia for fuel and other goods, but Russia also relies on

After the breakup of the Soviet Union, leaders of the former Soviet republics formed the Commonwealth of Independent States (CIS). The purpose of the organization is cooperation on regional issues such as trade and security, although to date the CIS has had few concrete accomplishments. Here, leaders of the CIS states (including Tajikistan's President Rahmonov, second from right) pose at a 2003 summit meeting.

Tajikistan's cotton. To ensure timely deliveries of this material, Russia has loaned the government money several times since the civil war, and in 2001 offered good terms for restructuring Tajikistan's $160 million debt.

President Rahmonov has reaffirmed the two countries' ties numerous times, and has called Russia Tajikistan's most reliable trading partner. But the countries' relations have not been without problems. In late 2002, Russia began deporting Tajikistanis, as well as immigrant workers from other Central Asian countries, saying they were in Russia illegally. The government of Tajikistan protested because tens of thousands of Tajikistanis count on money sent by immigrant workers in other countries for support each year. (According to a recent IMF estimate, citizens of Tajikistan working outside the country are expected to send approximately $200 million back to their families in 2004.) The immigration issue is not likely to be solved easily.

Central Asian Neighbors

The former Soviet republics have attempted to maintain good relations and work together on regional issues. All are members of the Commonwealth of Independent States, which was formed for this purpose. But since 1991 there have been several areas of tension in the relationships between Tajikistan and its neighbors.

Tajikistan and Kyrgyzstan share a border that was never officially agreed upon, and tensions over water led to a land dispute in 1989. Sporadic violence over the Isfara Valley continued until 1993. However, Kyrgyzstan sent medical supplies to help the wounded during Tajikistan's civil war and sent troops to help keep the peace after the fighting ended. Since then, the countries have signed several cooperative agreements and Kyrgyzstan opened an embassy in Dushanbe in 1997. Still, the presence of some 50,000 Tajik refugees in Kyrgyzstan has strained the countries' relations.

Tajikistan's relationship with Uzbekistan has also become strained. The countries are major trading partners—Uzbekistan buys about a quarter of Tajikistan's exports—and Uzbekistanis fought with pro-government forces during Tajikistan's civil war. However, the Uzbeks had backed a group of politicians who were maneuvered out of power by Rahmonov's hard-line faction. Relations worsened in 2000, when Uzbekistan decided to plant land mines along the countries' shared border. The government of Uzbekistan said it was trying to prevent members of the extremist Islamic Movement of Uzbekistan from crossing the border, which also is in dispute. Tajikistani officials say more than 60 civilians have been killed by the mines, and complain that Uzbekistani border guards wrongly detain Tajikistani nationals trying to cross legally between the countries.

Additionally, Uzbekistan has periodically held back fuel—natural gas, oil, and electricity—on which Tajikistan's economy depends, because of money Tajikistan owes it. At times, that debt has risen as high as $100 million.

In late 2003 and early 2004, officials from both nations held meetings to try to iron out some of these issues. As a result, Uzbekistan began sending more fuel to Tajikistan. After these talks, the media in both countries reported considerable improvement in the relationship. The governments of Tajikistan and Uzbekistan have also been talking about delineating a border they can agree on and removing the mines.

Rahmonov (left) shakes hands with Iranian President Mohammad Khatami (center) and Afghan leader Hamid Karzai after a 2003 meeting in Tehran. The three leaders signed an agreement to build a road from Iran's Persian Gulf coast to Tajikistan through Afghanistan.

All the countries in the region occasionally squabble over the use of water from the Amu and Syr rivers, which begin in the mountains and feed regional rivers in the countries. When the republics were under Soviet rule, government officials apportioned the water—as well as coal and oil—as needed. But now, no such regional overseer exists. Tajikistan and Kyrgyzstan get large amounts of water from the melting of the Pamir glaciers in the summer. But the water from those melts does not always reach Turkmenistan or Uzbekistan, and those countries need more water during summer months to irrigate their crops. Tajikistan controls the release of water from its Norak Dam—among the world's highest at 984 feet (300 m)—on the Vakhsh River. A hydroelectric power plant operates off the dam. If Tajikistan releases too little water from the Norak reservoir, crops suffer; if it releases too much, officials in Uzbekistan and Turkmenistan complain that downstream lands flood.

Because cotton is still among the region's most important crops and large amounts of water are needed to make cotton grow, water is constantly being diverted from the rivers to irrigate land. But the irrigation systems are now old and in need of repair, so a significant amount of water is wasted. Tajikistan and the other former Soviet republics have signed several water agreements to try to settle the matter, but the water use issue remains tense and unresolved.

Other Asian Neighbors

In 2002, Tajikistan and China finally settled a decades-long border dispute. China agreed to give up its claim to 10,800 square miles (28,000 sq km) of disputed territory on the border with Tajikistan; in return, Tajikistan ceded control over 386 square miles (1,000 sq km) of land in the Pamir Mountains to China, and the government agreed not to recognize Taiwan—which broke away from China in 1949—as an independent country. China is eager to "reunify" the country and exercise greater control over Taiwan, and it wants the backing of the international community in this effort.

China, which like the Soviet Union has a communist form of government, has also been battling against Muslim Uyghurs (or Uighurs), in its western Xinjiang autonomous province. Some Tajikistani Muslims living near the border are sympathetic to the separatists, but the Chinese government has asked Tajikistan to deny sanctuary to the rebels. Tajikistan and other Central Asian republics signed the 1996 Shanghai treaty, which demilitarized the borders, and the Dushanbe Declaration in 2000, in which they agreed to stop terrorism in the region. However, some observers fear that the signatory nations will use the latter treaty as a weapon to stifle opposition by stigmatizing any opposition as terrorist.

Iran has at times been interested in a closer relationship with the people to whom it has been historically linked, although Tajikistan has not been a high priority for the Iranian government. "From a geographical point of view, Tajikistan seems very remote from Iranian territory. But despite its physical distance, Iran is very sensitive to everything to do with Tajikistan, because of the cultural, historic and above all linguistic affinities between the two countries," wrote Mohammad-Reza Djalili and Frederic Grare in *Tajikistan: The Trials of Independence*. "From a political point of view, Iran does not wish to jeopardize its relations with Russia in any way by taking too high a profile in Tajik affairs. Tehran, perfectly aware of the pressure Moscow could still put on its borders, wants to maintain privileged links with a country which is one of its most important suppliers of arms and military materials."

Shortly after Tajikistan's independence, Iran became a market for the country's exports, particularly cotton and aluminum. It loaned Tajikistan money to improve its economy and agreed to pay some of Tajikistan's costs for importing natural gas in exchange for cotton. Iran also played a role in the peace process that ended the civil war of the mid-1990s.

In 1992, Tajikistan and several other former Soviet republics joined the Economic Cooperation Organization, which had been established in 1985 by Iran, Pakistan, and Turkey. That group's goals are to increase trade and improve regional economic growth. It also seeks to improve transportation and communication in and among members. However, not much had come of this effort by 2004.

Although the overthrow of Afghanistan's fundamentalist Taliban regime has made the government of Tajikistan feel more secure, officials remain concerned about drug smuggling, which originates in Afghanistan and cuts through Tajikistan on its way to Russia and Europe. In 2003 Tajikistani officials confiscated 6,100 pounds (2,773 kilograms) of drugs—80 percent of it heroin. Yet international agencies estimate that authorities are probably seizing only 10 percent of the drugs trafficked through the country.

The United States and other countries have recognized that stopping the drug trade will be an important element of waging war against international terrorism. As a result, the border with Afghanistan is heavily patrolled, and foreign aid has been sent to stop the illicit trade. Despite these efforts, smugglers have prospered. In its 2003 report *Tajikistan: A Roadmap to Development,* the Brussels-based International Crisis Group wrote, "Widespread poverty continues to fuel a major drug-trafficking business and provides potential breeding grounds for Islamist militant or other extremist groups. There is a strong international interest that Tajikistan avoid the fate of Afghanistan. Ignoring its very real problems would likely engender the conditions in which international terrorism and organized criminality thrive."

Relations with Europe and the United States

The countries of Europe generally have not gotten involved in Tajikistan's affairs. They have, however, been active in providing humanitarian aid to the country. Between 1992 and 2004, the European

Boxes of food donated by the United States await distribution in Dushanbe, circa 1992. During the 1990s, the U.S. gave humanitarian aid to Tajikistan to help the victims of the civil war, and also gave the government money to stop drug smuggling.

Commission (EC), the administrative arm of the European Union, gave $187.5 million in aid to Tajikistan. While money was used throughout the country, relief efforts were concentrated particularly in the Khatlon region, which has been the poorest. The money from the European Commission was used for food, improving water pumping stations to provide clean water to more people, providing medical supplies and medicines, training medical staff, and distributing mosquito netting to help prevent malaria. However, in 2004 the EC announced it will gradually phase out humanitarian aid to focus more on its development programs.

After Tajikistan became independent, the United States made a limited effort to establish trade. In 1994, the United States established the Central Asian-American Enterprise Fund to provide loans and technical assistance to the former Soviet republics of Central Asia to foster economic growth. During the 1990s the U.S. also provided humanitarian aid and funds to help Tajikistan's drug interdiction efforts.

Things changed after the terrorist attack on the United States in September 2001. Tajikistan's government was quick to support the U.S. efforts against the Taliban. Tajikistan hosted troops working with the U.S.-led coalition, allowed military planes to fly through its airspace, and gave U.S., British, and French forces access to its airbases, as well as the international airport at Dushanbe.

As a result, relations between the U.S. and Tajikistan have improved. High-ranking American officials have visited Tajikistan, and in 2002 President Rahmonov visited Washington, D.C., and met with U.S. President George W. Bush. The amount of U.S. aid to Tajikistan, especially for security purposes, has increased. In 2001, the United States gave Tajikistan about $67 million; the next year that figure increased to about $138 million, including "emergency terrorism supplemental appropriations." The aid has not all been for military support or drug interdiction efforts, however. Project HOPE, a nongovernmental program sponsored by the Department of State, provided $57 million in medical supplies between 2002 and 2004. Aid has also focused on economic reconstruction in the country, and the U.S. government has given small grants to nongovernmental organizations working on such issues as improving democracy and fostering free speech through mass media. And it has donated dozens of vehicles and thousands of uniforms to border officials.

In addition, the United States committed to spending as much as $40 million to build a bridge between Tajikistan and Afghanistan over the Panj (Piandzh) River. The 2,200-foot-long (670-meter-long) bridge will re-open a trade route. U.S. officials also performed the necessary hydrological and topographical preparatory work.

Although the United States established diplomatic relations with Tajikistan by early 1992, in 1998 the U.S. embassy, which was located on one floor of a downtown hotel in Dushanbe, was closed because of security concerns. For the next several years the U.S. embassy operated out of Almaty, Kazakhstan, but by 2005 the U.S. was looking for a secure site to open a new embassy in the capital of Tajikistan.

With regard to foreign relations, Rahmonov seems to be keeping all options open. In an address to parliament in April 2002, he talked about the importance of the country's strong relationship with Russia. But Rahmonov also said Tajikistan should use the aftermath of the September 11 attacks to establish closer ties with the United States and other western countries. After this, Pravda and other Russian news services contended that Tajikistan's stronger relationship with the U.S. was straining its ties with Russia.

Continued involvement by the United States, accompanied by increased aid and greater trade, could reduce some of the influence Russia has over Tajikistan. Tajikistan needs to take the help it is receiving from powerful countries all over the world, and use it to restructure its economy to provide a better life for its people. More than anything else, that should help preserve the tenuous peace among the various factions within the country.

6th century B.C.:	Achaemenid Persian domination of Central Asia begins.
334 B.C.:	Alexander the Great invades Persia and begins his conquest of Central Asia.
8th century A.D.:	Invading Arabs introduce Islam to Central Asia.
875:	Samanids take control of the region, ruling first from Samarqand and later from Bukhara.
994:	Abulqasem Firdawsi finishes *Shohnoma* (or *Shah-Nameh* in Persian), a history of Iran's rulers deemed a vital part of Tajikistan's literary heritage and that of Persian speakers elsewhere.
1219:	Genghis Khan and the Mongols invade Central Asia.
1370:	This period starts the domination of Timur Lenk, who rebuilt Samarqand and over the next 35 years established a vast empire in Asia.
1500s:	The Turkic dynasty of the Shaybanids (Shabanids) rules the region.
1613:	The Romanov dynasty is established in Russia.
1866:	Russia annexes Khujand and Uroteppa, both in modern-day Tajikistan.
1868:	The emirate of Bukhara is made a Russian protectorate.
1895:	Russia and Great Britain agree on borders in Central Asia.
1912:	The first newspaper in the Tajik language is published near Bukhara.

Chronology

1916:	Citizen rebellion against Russian rule breaks out in Khujand.
1917:	Faced by widespread revolt in Russia, in March Czar Nicholas II abdicates and a republic is formed; in November Vladimir Lenin leads the Bolshevik revolution, starting a civil war.
1918:	The Basmachi opposition movement begins in Tajikistan.
1921:	Dushanbe is captured by Bolshevik forces and Northern Tajikistan is made part of the Turkestan Soviet Socialist Republic.
1922:	The Union of Soviet Socialist Republics is created.
1924:	Soviets delineate new borders in Central Asia, including Tajikistan as an autonomous region within Uzbekistan.
1929:	The Tajik Soviet Socialist Republic is created.
1930s:	Following the forced resettlement of numerous villages, the Soviets begin widespread cultivation of the land to increase cotton production in Tajikistan.
1932:	Soviet forces defeat the last of the Basmachi.
1940:	The alphabet of the written Tajik language is changed from Latin to Cyrillic.
1949:	An earthquake leaves 29,000 dead and decimates 150 villages.
1951:	The Academy of Sciences in Tajikistan is created.
1960:	Soviets build the world's largest hydroelectric dam on the Vakhsh River at Norak.

1985: Mikhail Gorbachev becomes the head of the Soviet Union and ushers in a new era of openness called *glasnost*.

1989: Tajik is declared the official language by the Supreme Soviet of Tajikistan.

1991: An attempted coup against Gorbachev is unsuccessful, hastening the collapse of the Soviet Union; Tajikistan declares its independence, and Rahmon Nabiev is elected the country's first president; Tajikistan joins with Russia in the Commonwealth of Independent States (CIS).

1992: Civil war begins in Tajikistan; a Government of National Reconciliation is formed; Nabiev is forced to resign; the Supreme Soviet abolishes the presidency and chooses Imomali Rahmonov as Tajikistan's leader.

1993: Opposition parties are banned; Russia and Tajikistan sign the Agreement on Friendship, Cooperation, and Mutual Assistance; CIS peacekeepers are sent to guard the Tajikistan-Afghan border.

1994: Opposing sides agree to a cease-fire and peace talks begin; voters approve a new constitution reestablishing the presidency and electing Rahmonov to the office.

1997: The civil war ends with the signing of a peace accord in Moscow by government officials and the United Tajik Opposition; Rahmonov is hurt in a grenade attack but not seriously injured.

1998: Rahmonov pardons all exiled opposition leaders; four United Nations military observers are murdered.

Chronology

1999:	The countries sign an agreement to allow Russia to build a military base in Tajikistan; the United Tajik Opposition ends its armed opposition activites; Rahmonov is reelected president; parliament agrees to allow Russian troops to stay in Tajikistan.
2000:	The somoni becomes the new national currency.
2001:	Assassins kill Tajikistan's deputy interior minister; Rahmonov announces Tajikistan's support for the U.S. war against the Taliban in Afghanistan, after terrorist attacks on the United States kill nearly 3,000.
2002:	The number of border guards doubles to prevent al-Qaeda members from escaping from Afghanistan.
2003:	Crackdowns lead to the arrests of numerous people accused of being Islamic militants, including the deputy leader of the opposition Islamic Renaissance Party, who is charged with murder; a referendum that will permit Rahmonov to run for two more seven-year terms is approved.
2004:	Russia begins to withdraw its guards from the Tajikistan-Afghanistan border; they are replaced by the Border Guard of Tajikistan.
2005:	The People's Democratic Party of Tajikistan wins 52 of 63 seats in parliamentary elections. The United States and the Organization for Security and Cooperation in Europe agree that the vote failed to meet international standards of fairness.

arable—land capable of growing crops.

authoritarian—a government in which a small group exercises the authority.

Basmachi—literally "robbers," this was the derogatory name given to the peasants who rebelled against Soviet rule in Tajikistan in the 1920s.

Bolshevik—the radical Russian party led by Vladimir Lenin that seized power in 1917 and established the Soviet Union.

Cyrillic—the Russian alphabet, which is still commonly used in Tajikistan.

deforestation—the clearing of trees from a forest.

desertification—the process through which land becomes a desert, usually due to a combination of drought and the overuse of the land.

glacier—a large ice mass formed by snowfall over time that spreads slowly outward.

gross domestic product (GDP)—the total value of all goods and services produced within a country in a year.

mudflow—a movement of earth, debris, and water.

Qur'an—the holy book of Islam that was revealed to Muhammad in the seventh century.

Ramadan—the ninth month of the Islamic lunar calendar, during which Muslims fast from sunrise to sunset.

Taliban—the Islamist ruling regime of Afghanistan that came to power in the mid-1990s. The Taliban was accused of protecting Osama bin Laden and his al-Qaeda terrorist organization, and was overthrown by a U.S.-led invasion of Afghanistan in late 2001.

viloyat—the name for a province in Tajikistan.

Further Reading

Abdullaev, Kamoludin, and Shahram Akbarzadeh. *Historical Dictionary of Tajikistan*. Lanham, Md.: The Scarecrow Press, 2002.

Cartlidge, Cherese, and Charles Clark. *The Central Asian States*. San Diego: Lucent Books, 2001.

Curtis, Glenn E. *Kazakhstan, Kyrgyzstan, Tajikistan, Turkmenistan and Uzbekistan Country Studies*. Washington, D.C.: U.S. Government Printing Office, 1997.

Kort, Michael G. *The Handbook of the Former Soviet Union*. Brookfield, Conn.: Millbrook Press, 1997.

Major, John S., and Betty Belarus. *Caravan to America: Living Arts of the Silk Road*. Chicago: Cricket Books, 2002.

Meyer, Karl E. *The Dust of Empire: The Race for Mastery in the Asian Heartland*. New York: Public Affairs, 2003.

———. *Tournament of Shadows: The Great Game and Race for Empire in Central Asia*. New York: Counterpoint, 1999.

Rashid, Ahmed. *Jihad: The Rise of Militant Islam in Central Asia*. New Haven, Conn.: Yale University Press, 2002.

Shoumatoff, Nicholas, and Nina Shoumatoff, eds. *Around the Roof of the World*. Ann Arbor: University of Michigan Press, 2000.

Whitlock, Monica. *Land Beyond the River: The Untold Story of Central Asia*. New York: Thomas Dunne Books, 2003.

http://www.cia.gov/cia/publications/factbook/geos/ti.html

The website for the CIA World Factbook entry on Tajikistan includes statistics and facts about the country.

http://www.angelfire.com/sd/tajikistanupdate/#nw

The Tajikistan Update provides information on culture and travel, plus links to many other resources.

http://www.reliefweb.int/w/rwb.nsf/vCD/Tajikistan?OpenDocum ent&StartKey=Tajikistan&ExpandView

This website, part of Relief Web, provides access to documents about humanitarian and disaster-relief efforts in Tajikistan.

http://tajikistan.tajnet.com/english/news.htm

The official website for the government of Tajikistan includes news and information about the country's geography, culture, economy, and structure of government.

http://news.bbc.co.uk/1/hi/world/asia-pacific/country_pro- files/1296639.stm

Background information on Tajikistan provided by the British Broadcasting Corporation (BBC).

http://www.grida.no/enrin/soe.cfm?country=TJ

The website for Tajikistan, sponsored by the Central and Eastern Europe, Caucasus and Central Asia Environmental Information Program, provides details about the state of the country's environment.

http://hrw.org/doc/?t=europe&c=tajiki

This Human Rights Watch website gives information about the state of human rights in Tajikistan.

Index

Numbers in **bold italic** refer to captions.

Index

Picture Credits

The **FOREIGN POLICY RESEARCH INSTITUTE (FPRI)** served as editorial consultants for the GROWTH AND INFLUENCE OF ISLAM IN THE NATIONS OF ASIA AND CENTRAL ASIA series. FPRI is one of the nation's oldest "think tanks." The Institute's Middle East Program focuses on Gulf security, monitors the Arab-Israeli peace process, and sponsors an annual conference for teachers on the Middle East, plus periodic briefings on key developments in the region.

Among the FPRI's trustees is a former Secretary of State and a former Secretary of the Navy (and among the FPRI's former trustees and interns, two current Undersecretaries of Defense), not to mention two university presidents emeritus, a foundation president, and several active or retired corporate CEOs.

The scholars of FPRI include a former aide to three U.S. Secretaries of State, a Pulitzer Prize–winning historian, a former president of Swarthmore College and a Bancroft Prize–winning historian, and two former staff members of the National Security Council. And the FPRI counts among its extended network of scholars— especially its Inter-University Study Groups—representatives of diverse disciplines, including political science, history, economics, law, management, religion, sociology, and psychology.

DR. HARVEY SICHERMAN is president and director of the Foreign Policy Research Institute in Philadelphia, Pennsylvania. He has extensive experience in writing, research, and analysis of U.S. foreign and national security policy, both in government and out. He served as Special Assistant to Secretary of State Alexander M. Haig Jr. and as a member of the Policy Planning Staff of Secretary of State James A. Baker III. Dr. Sicherman was also a consultant to Secretary of the Navy John F. Lehman Jr. (1982–1987) and Secretary of State George Shultz (1988).

A graduate of the University of Scranton (B.S., History, 1966), Dr. Sicherman earned his Ph.D. at the University of Pennsylvania (Political Science, 1971), where he received a Salvatori Fellowship. He is author or editor of numerous books and articles, including *America the Vulnerable: Our Military Problems and How to Fix Them* (FPRI, 2002) and *Palestinian Autonomy, Self-Government and Peace* (Westview Press, 1993). He edits *Peacefacts*, an FPRI bulletin that monitors the Arab-Israeli peace process.

COLLEEN O'DEA has been a journalist for 22 years. She received a 2002–03 Journalism Fellowship in Child and Family Policy through the University of Maryland. She has won numerous journalism awards from such organizations as the New Jersey Press Association, Gannett, and the Casey Journalism Center. In 2004, she was a member of a team of Gannett New Jersey reporters whose series "Profiting from Public Service" won several national awards, including the Selden Ring for investigative reporting, the National Headliner Award for public service journalism, and the Ursula and Dr. Gilbert Farfel Prize for Excellence in Investigative Reporting.

O'Dea lives in High Bridge, New Jersey, with her husband, Paul Wyckoff, and sons William and Kevin. She is grateful they gave her the space and support to write this book.